Melissa offers herself as a fearle... [P9-DTD-563] ...d gives us this compassionate book about her own journey into the dark to serve as handrails for those of us who find ourselves, willingly or not, descending into the underworlds of depression, pain, anxiety, and beyond to find the riches they hide.

Jason Gray, singer and songwriter

Melissa's voice and story bear witness to the reality that the Christian narrative doesn't always follow the path of celebration and triumph. For those of us whose lives are a testament to darkness, suffering and survival, we too need to be reminded that our stories also belong to those of the family of God. *The Radiant Midnight* does this beautifully and honestly, offering compassionate and challenging insights along the way.

David C. Wang, ThM, PhD, associate professor of psychology, Biola University;
pastor of spiritual formation, One Life City Church

As a woman who has experienced a good bit of her life in the midnight hours, I'm grateful for another voice that tenderly and candidly calls attention to a subject many Christians have ignored. Melissa doesn't just set the subject in front of you—she digs deep and encourages you to push harder against the darkness than you may have ever dared to do.

Angie Smith, bestselling author of *Seamless, Chasing God,* and *What Women Fear*

I so appreciate Melissa Maimone's honesty and unique perspective on battling depression and anxiety. She skillfully weaves King David's life and words with her own, giving the reader space to battle fear, worry, and heavy sadness—yet with hope. If you're facing your own midnight, find solace and light in these hard-won words.

Mary DeMuth, author of *Healing Every Day*

"Radiant midnight" is an oxymoron—a combination of two contradictory terms that invite a curious mind to explore the wisdom that might hold them together. In this way, "radiant midnight" now establishes its place in a lexicon that has illuminated other impossible truths like "sweet sorrow," "wounded healer," or "terrible goodness." Through her achingly personal journey, Melissa sets the night on fire with the radiance of unrelenting love, revealing what we can never see or feel when we are in the dark—God is already there.

Nicole Johnson, author of *Creating Calm in the Center of Crazy* and *Fresh Brewed Life*; founder of Seasons Weekends

Melissa doesn't hand out Band-Aids or tidy answers. Rather, she invites us to listen for the story of redemption that God is writing for each of us, even as we wait for the light.

Jen Wise, author of *The Bright Life*

Melissa's attempt to put her experience into words is both a gift and treasure for any reader. Her vulnerability reveals a bold, courageous woman whose aim is to ensure that you, the reader, do not have to walk your journey alone.

Andrea Tomassi, author of *Live Bold*

Like a good therapist, Melissa sits with you in your pain and teaches you how to sit with your own darkness. This book speaks to anyone who struggles with any type of darkness in their life—and that would be all of us! She so accurately and vulnerably portrays the shame of the shadow that most of us feel but can never put into words. But instead of condemnation, Melissa gives a wonderful combination of humor, heart, and hope in the darkest times.

Dr. Zoe Shaw, host of *The Dr. Zoe Show* podcast

If you are suffering, this book is a safe space. Melissa isn't here to fix you or your feelings. Rather, she masterfully weaves Scripture, personal stories, and profound insights to offer you eternal hope that is both raw and real. As one who currently sits in the long, dark days of a midnight season, *The Radiant Midnight* stirred my resolve to learn to sit and learn God's lessons rather than try to speed through the pain.

Barb Roose, author of *Winning the Worry Battle*

Melissa's vulnerability, humor, and depth make her one of our favorite voices to hear on some of life's harder topics. Her story and wisdom have helped illuminate the treasure to be found in our own dark places.

Katherine and Jay Wolf, coauthors and cofounders of Hope Heals

The
RADIANT
Midnight

MELISSA MAIMONE

HARVEST HOUSE PUBLISHERS
EUGENE, OREGON

Unless otherwise indicated, all Scripture quotations are taken from the Holy Bible, New International Version®, NIV®. Copyright © 1973, 1978, 1984, 2011 by Biblica, Inc.® Used by permission. All rights reserved worldwide.

Verses marked ESV are from The ESV® Bible (The Holy Bible, English Standard Version®), copyright © 2001 by Crossway, a publishing ministry of Good News Publishers. Used by permission. All rights reserved.

Verses marked MSG are taken from THE MESSAGE, copyright © 1993, 1994, 1995, 1996, 2000, 2001, 2002 by Eugene H. Peterson. Used by permission of NavPress. All rights reserved. Represented by Tyndale House Publishers, Inc.

Verses marked NCV are taken from the New Century Version®. Copyright © 2005 by Thomas Nelson, Inc. Used by permission. All rights reserved.

Verses marked NLT are taken from the Holy Bible, New Living Translation, copyright © 1996, 2004, 2015 by Tyndale House Foundation. Used by permission of Tyndale House Publishers, Inc., Carol Stream, Illinois 60188. All rights reserved.

Verses marked TLB are taken from The Living Bible copyright © 1971. Used by permission of Tyndale House Publishers, Inc., Carol Stream, Illinois 60188. All rights reserved.

Cover design by Faceout Studio

Cover photos © Ana Babii, OLaLa Merkel / Shutterstock

The Radiant Midnight
Copyright © 2019 by Melissa Maimone
Published by Harvest House Publishers
Eugene, Oregon 97408
www.harvesthousepublishers.com

ISBN 978-0-7369-7647-3 (Trade)
ISBN 978-0-7369-7648-0 (eBook)

Library of Congress Cataloging-in-Publication Data is on file at the Library of Congress, Washington, DC

All rights reserved. No part of this publication may be reproduced, stored in a retrieval system, or transmitted in any form or by any means—electronic, mechanical, digital, photocopy, recording, or any other—except for brief quotations in printed reviews, without the prior permission of the publisher.

Printed in the United States of America
19 20 21 22 23 24 25 26 27 / BP-GL / 10 9 8 7 6 5 4 3 2 1

To those longing for the light to return.
You are not alone in the darkness.

CONTENTS

FOREWORD

Curt Thompson, MD

The first time I heard Melissa Maimone speak publicly about her story of affliction, I was immediately captivated. She spoke with authority—as one who *authors*. As one who was offering something that was emerging from the center of her soul, not something she had read about on the Internet. She spoke not as one who was talking from a distance about some *thing*, but rather as one bearing faithful witness to her journey—true to its complete nature of joy and heartache, beauty and anguish, light and darkness. She told of her experience of depression not as something apart from herself, but rather as an integral element of her life—threads that God was patiently weaving into a tapestry of such elegance and refinement that one could not help but be drawn into it. At its deepest level, her story was my own. I am confident that in *The Radiant Midnight* you will find your own as well.

For nearly 30 years I have practiced as a psychiatrist. My most important calling is to walk with people into places in their stories that they have not yet traveled. Their reluctance to have traversed these paths—whether consciously or not—has led them to any number of painful realities that have them on the brink. They are usually attempting to regulate states of depression, anxiety, substance (or other) addictions, broken relationships of all kinds, and any number of other emotional and behavioral maladies. At the heart of their troubles lie, among other things, their inexperience at telling their stories fully in all of their agonizing, shaming, beautiful grandeur. They have not the words to say—or the person to *hear* them say—that which is truest about who they are and what they are enduring.

This deeply entrenched reality—our inability to tell the truth about who we are—is as old as humanity. In our present day, this has led to an avalanche of mental health needs as the increase in rates of depression, anxiety, addiction, and suicide show no signs of relenting.

As a neuroscientist who speaks frequently about research discoveries relating to the interplay between the brain and relationships, you would think I would be the supreme optimist. And indeed, I am grateful for and hopeful about what we are learning about rewiring our minds. But it is not enough for us to have more new information in the information age. Rather, we need embodied evidence that our lives can change, that our minds can be renewed, and that joy can be known—not just as a *result of* but even *in the face of* darkness. We don't just need better stories; we need truer stories. Stories that tell of a God who meets us in order to save us and extend the boundaries of our imaginations beyond the horizons we can see. I mostly *want* a God who will transform my darkness while leaving me alone and not asking me to change that much. But it turns out that far more often what I *need*—and what I get—is a God who transforms me *through* that darkness. Unfortunately, we suffer from a dearth of stories telling us that this is how God frequently works.

Into this breach—this chasm that lies between the God of our midnights and our belief that there should be no such darkness at all—steps our author. And she knows of what she speaks. She speaks of the gifts of surrender and suffering; of time and silence;

of community, courage, and hope. There is the invitation to solitude where God can find us in all of our shameful, glorious, broken, beautiful selves. For her, midnight is not something that is primarily to be escaped; it is that which God is using to—often to my utter incomprehension and resistance—love us.

And as she writes, our author does not flinch. She denies not one square inch of painful terrain that we all must cover if we are the least bit serious about following Jesus. But Melissa rightly reflects that this suffering—this midnight—is the very thing that God is using to transform us into creatures we will barely recognize once the process is complete. She covers this ground so effectively that by the time you have read the final page you will have few questions about how the gifts about which she speaks are indeed that—gifts.

But there is something more. In *The Radiant Midnight* you will find not merely abstract ideas about the essence of darkness or how to go about facing it. You will also find humor. Wisdom. Honesty. You will find Melissa's very bone and blood. You will find a style of writing that draws you into the text because it is the sound of Melissa's voice. A voice of kindness and grace. A voice of relentless and comprehensive transparency. A voice that speaks not just *to* you but *for* you, the reader, the things you have felt and sensed and known to be true but have not yet found the words or the way. She can do this because she is herself immersed in the very work she invites you to join her in doing. She is no stranger to anything about which she speaks. She will not ask you to do something she herself has not been willing to pay the price for.

And it is here, then, in reading—rather, perhaps, listening to—her words, that your heart, trapped as it may feel in its own midnight, begins to see the first signs of dawn. Light that is not an indication that your affliction is summarily resolved, but that confidently assures you that in your darkness, God does not, will not, leave you alone, but is truly in the business of revealing His works and your glory in the depth of your travail. This, my fellow traveler, is something that often requires great patience but is God's way of disclosing what it means to practice for His new heaven and earth that are surely coming.

And so, I commend this book to you and to anyone you know who, having read it, will be as grateful as I am that Melissa has written it. Grateful for a God who in the depth of our midnights sees only radiance. And will stop at nothing until we not only see the same but have become that very thing.

Curt Thompson, MD
Author of *Anatomy of the Soul* and *The Soul of Shame*

INTRODUCTION

Night, do your gentle work; in you I put my trust.

<small>Dietrich Bonhoeffer[1]</small>

I t was 1999 when the darkness descended again. I was a happily married wife and mother of two, surrounded by wonderful friends and a good church. I had a strong foundation of faith. There was no reasonable explanation for the dread I felt upon waking every morning and the sense of isolation and despair that edged its way into my increasingly scattered thoughts. I couldn't seem to pull it together, no matter how hard I tried. In desperation, I sought out a Christian counselor with the hope that he could talk me out of my unmitigated sadness.

I slumped into his chair, tissues in hand, tears rolling down my face, apologetically explaining that I was falling apart without any earthly reason to do so. I exclaimed, "I believe in Jesus. Everything changed when I gave my life to Him! I love Him! I love my life! So what is wrong with me?" After questioning me about my physical health, my daily routines, and my energy level, my new therapist suggested perhaps I was suffering from depression. Furthermore, he recommended medication. "Have you been diagnosed with depression before?" he asked gently. I hung my head in shame. "Yes," I whispered.

I had been a Christian for about four years when that conversation with my counselor took place. It was the first time I experienced the darkness of depression after becoming a believer in Jesus Christ. It would not be the last. I've battled anxiety and depression for most of my life. It has come and gone through the years, but like cobwebs that show up in the corners of my house, the darkness always returns. Though I've given my life to Christ, the peace of God that surpasses understanding (Philippians 4:7) can elude me. Though I work in ministry, I often cannot minister to my own soul. Though I turn to the Bible regularly, the words do not penetrate the sorrow that can live bone-deep inside of me. My marriage is satisfying, my friendships dear, my children healthy, and yet none of these relationships completely alleviates my loneliness.

I hated being depressed. I fought it. I felt deep shame about it. This formidable presence bullied every area of my life. Depression pushed around my marriage. It undermined my passion for the church. It chipped away at my faith. Its presence in my life made absolutely no sense. How could I serve God's people when I was afraid to talk to them? How could I lead when I was overwhelmed by feelings of inadequacy and doubt? How was I to be strong when I felt so fragile? How could I take proper care of my children when I could barely get out of bed? If I was called to be a light in this world, why was I helpless to shake the darkness in my own heart?

In my appeals to the Lord, I made dramatic courtroom arguments. I told Him how impractical it all was. I told Him He was making a huge mistake. I explained how granting my request for relief would be beneficial for both of us. I flailed my arms around and used impressive, fabulous words in order to convince Him to take the depression and sadness away. I *rocked* those arguments. Even so, God didn't budge.

In a letter to the Corinthian church, the apostle Paul explores his own deep pain. In many Bible translations, it's referred to as a "thorn" in the flesh (2 Corinthians 12:7) But in the original Greek, the word Paul uses for "thorn" is *skolops*, which more literally translated means stake[2]; like the kind you drive into the ground or those guys in the movies use to kill vampires. His impairment was more than a slight prick of the finger. Paul was stabbed by it. He was debilitated because of it, and he asked God to take it away three times. In response to Paul's courtroom arguments God replied, "My grace is sufficient for you, for my power is made perfect in weakness" (2 Corinthians 12:9). In other words, the answer is, "No, I will not take it away. I've got this and you've got Me. That is enough." Like Paul, I asked the God I love and trust to take away this painful stake buried deep in my flesh. And like Paul, the Lord responded with a loving but firm, "No. You've got Me. I will be enough for you."

I believe with all my being that God can heal me, which makes the no all the more painful. I've wondered if God is holding out on me. Like a teasing adult waving a piece of candy above a child's head, my desire is within sight but out of reach. Yet I also believe we have a God whose love is so high, so wide, and so deep we couldn't see its edges if looking through the Hubble Space Telescope. Out of these beliefs—and really, if I am honest, out of sheer exhaustion—I took a radical step: I stopped fighting the darkness. I decided that if my depression has been permitted by the God who loves me completely, then perhaps my focus on removing it distracts me from why He left it there in the first place.

For the first time, I looked at my stake closely. I bent down and turned my head to study it. I tried to see it from all angles, but because it's a part of me, I have only partial perspective. Nevertheless, over the years I've poked and prodded and run my fingers along its rough edges and smooth indentations. Because I'm less afraid of the splintery darkness that takes over my heart and mind, I'm more comfortable contemplating its purpose. And here's what I've come to believe: My afflictions are not God's punishment or cruel game. He is not oblivious or inattentive to my suffering. The stake planted in my flesh is allowed to remain there because God offers His grace instead. He knows my soul needs it more than healing, even when I would argue otherwise. My deepest wounds are invitations to explore the aspects of God that scare me most: His power, His holiness, and His ways, which are so unlike mine. Through my explorations, among my questions and rants and tears, my perspective on the broken places in my soul has changed. I've come to believe the darkness has more to offer than just pain.

No one gets through this life unscathed by suffering, loss, or heartache. You probably have issues that recur just when you are sure you've finally moved past them. Like a thorn (or stake) that refuses to budge from your side, some days (or months or years) these issues ache and at other times lie dormant. Either way, they never quite disappear. Perhaps it's grief. Maybe it's a difficult marriage. It could be an eating disorder or an addiction or even a crisis of faith. Maybe, like me, you struggle with depression. It might not be anything that requires a diagnosis or is even tangible enough to describe. Whatever the details of your story, you've ended up here in the dark. You've found yourself in unfamiliar surroundings, without direction, without light, without an exit. You stretch out your hands and grope around in desperation; all you know for sure is that you want out of this murky, awful place.

Avoiding pain and wanting relief as soon as possible is only natural. It might feel like this place of darkness is yours alone to experience because you can't see anyone (or anything) else. Sometimes you can't hear anything either, because when we are afraid and want to escape, most of us thrash around quite a bit. With all the panicked crashing and banging and blind desperation, we miss the goodness the dark places have to offer.

But if you quiet your soul just a bit and rest your body for a while,

I believe you will hear the voice of the One who loves you most. He is the One who sings songs of love over you. He is the One who has invited you to a life that relies on more than sight or circumstance. And I believe with all my heart this darkness allowed by God is an invitation to those He dearly loves to discover His powerful grace in unexpected places.

Through trial and error, panic and faith, tears and blessing, I've begun to understand how to rest in the darkness. I've learned to embrace the things I wanted God to remove most. It has not always been a pretty sight, but it's happened. I've spent some time here, and my eyes have adjusted to the darkness a bit, so grab my hand and we can go together. Let's explore this uncomfortable place where we don't want to be. We will go slowly, because if we run in the dark, we will bump our shins and scrape our knees. It's easy to trip and fall when you can't see what's in front of you. I've got the scars to prove it.

In the course of this book, we will walk step by step into this journey of surrender, suffering, rest, and restoration. We will explore shadowy places, but we will not be alone. Jesus Christ, the lover of our soul and the lifter of our head, will be there too. And in the silence of Midnight, when eyes no longer see and ears are attuned, we will discover God's gifts in the dark places.

1

WELCOME TO MIDNIGHT

In choosing to face the night, I took the first steps toward sunrise.

Gerald L. Sittser[1]

I've always assumed the main purpose of suffering is to be victorious over it. None of us welcome discomfort or invite it to linger. The natural response to pain is to extricate yourself from it as soon as possible. The harsher the pain, the more rapidly we pray to God for relief. Suffering is often viewed as a speed bump on the road to victorious living. It couldn't possibly be an intended destination, could it? Following Christ is more appealing when you are moving toward a "city on a hill" than the garden of Gethsemane.

John of the Cross was a sixteenth-century Spanish mystic who was convinced suffering was not only part of the Christian life but necessary for spiritual maturity. He believed in order to purify and refine faith, one must go through the process of losing, at least for a time, any sense of God's presence. He saw significance in souls who cry out to a God they cannot feel or see. He encouraged people to embrace discomfort.

Church authorities responded to his ideas by throwing him in

prison. They apparently didn't take to the notion that pain is important. But confinement only fueled John's beliefs. From a cell so small
he couldn't stand up straight, he wrote poems and prose about faith
and suffering and the way of the cross.[2] He put words to the dis-
tress we can feel so deeply that it soaks into the marrow of our bones.

What name would you give to a time of suffering so bleak and
black that you stumble around in disoriented terror? What encapsulates the experience of enduring deep sorrows while trying to hold
on to the One who overcame them? John of the Cross called it the
"dark night of the soul."[3] I call it "Midnight."

Only three things named in Scripture are present before the
beginning of the world: God, water, and darkness. The Message
translation of Scripture describes it like this: "Earth was a soup
of nothingness, a bottomless emptiness, an inky blackness. God's
Spirit brooded like a bird above the watery abyss" (Genesis 1:2). The
Lord's first glorious act of creation was to split that inky blackness
with radiance. He proclaimed, "Let there be light" (Genesis 1:3) and
there was. It was like a powerful drumbeat at the beginning of a new
song; a pounding cadence building into a full-blown symphony of
plants, flowers, animals, and unabashed beauty. He separated the
light and the darkness, and with that the rhythm of the whole earth
commenced. He named those earliest drumbeats day and night,
and Midnight was given a specific, intentional place in the world.

The Israelites understood the night. They knew it was just as
ordained and ordered by God as the daytime.[4] They believed, as
David says in Psalm 139:12, "Even the darkness will not be dark to
you; the night will shine like the day, for darkness is as light to you."
While darkness and night are viewed at times with foreboding in
Scripture, God's people are assured of His power and control over it.

Midnight has an important place in the universe. It brings the
moon, which is crucial to the rhythm of the oceans, the orbit of the

earth, and the change of seasons. It offers stars that orient travelers on both sea and land to their place in the universe and to future destinations. It marks the end of one day and ushers in the beginning of another. Midnight is quieter than daytime. Birds fall silent and crickets sing instead. Flowers close and the air cools. Midnight is made for rest, waiting, and stillness. Even if you have someone sleeping next to you, Midnight can be a solitary time.

In the midst of affliction, a Midnight of the soul invites darkness and silence too. Hebrews 11:1 states: "Now faith is confidence in what we hope for and assurance about what we do not see." At Midnight your eyes fail, forcing your ears to take over and do the heavy lifting. While this is not always beneficial to feeling safe and in control, there is something important about learning to use your eyes less and your ears more. You become attuned and aware of your surroundings in a new way. And the best part of Midnight? It promises morning.

I like mornings. I like coffee, breakfast burritos, and donuts. I like having the entire day in front of me, full of potential and plans and productivity. Who doesn't? No one likes to feel blind and vulnerable, groping around for something to hold on to. So it makes sense that we focus a lot of energy on how to get out of our Midnights and into the mornings where we can see what is before us.

And yet I've spent a lot of time in Midnight. To believe its main purpose was simply to get me back to daylight is disquieting. I don't want to take the hardest parts of my life and put them behind me just because they are painful. I want to find out why God has allowed them. I want to lean in and use my eyes less and my ears more so I might become attuned to His still, small voice whispering the story of redemption. I need to know that, true to Psalm 56:8 (NLT), the Lord has collected all my tears in a bottle and that nothing has been wasted. I am desperate to understand the things that have brought so much confusion to my heart. I need to know that

God's grace is not diminished in the midst of affliction. Because if the darkest times of my life have less significance than the brightest times, then a lot of life is lost to hopelessness.

God has allowed the darkness as surely as He proclaimed, "Let there be light" (Genesis 1:3). He has purpose for every part of your existence. He is never confused. He is never lost. He wastes nothing. He is the God of the seasons, the moon, and the seas. Therefore, Midnight is His as well. And so are you.

Whether we are in a dark season now or have been in the past, the good news is that there are things to be discovered in Midnight that will bring comfort, peace, and ultimately an abiding hope to our deepest pain. Mature faith is mostly developed in the dark. The marvelous, heartbreaking, brilliant, and excruciating work of Midnight is sacred and ordained. It is allowed, blessed, and overseen by a God who loves us enough to do His refining. To be sure, the work we are called to do at Midnight is important. But it is very different from our daylight work.

Daylight Work

Daylight work is when you put your strengths and gifts to full use. It originates in natural abilities and talents and is often accompanied by particular gifts of the Spirit that are ordained as faith develops. When you are doing your daylight work, you are acknowledging and using your particular attributes that bless others and reflect God. It is God's invitation to partner with Him in the work of reaching His people. Each of us has been given a unique set of talents and we are called to use them. It's how you shine in this world. Your daylight work incorporates all the ways you show up to this life and bless others.

Some people do their daylight work within the walls of the church. Pastors, volunteers, administrators, and Sunday school teachers use their gifts specifically to grow and bless a congregation. But daylight work is certainly not limited to religious organizations. You can be a car mechanic, Realtor, basket weaver, or spreadsheet maker and be doing your daylight work. Your career is part of your offering to the world. This is fantastic because you get the added benefit of receiving a paycheck for your daylight work. But even if it's not a paying gig, your strengths and gifts have immense value. Making a fantastic dinner or planting a garden or helping out in your community blesses people.

Moreover, daylight work is not just about being good at things. It's about who you are as a person; it capitalizes on the ways you have been "fearfully and wonderfully made" (Psalm 139:14). Daylight work reflects the mature and developed aspects of your character. It is the part of your personality that comes naturally and is in line with the character of God. It could be the knack for making a stranger feel welcome. It might be down-to-earth humor that lightens a mood at just the right moment. It can be a quiet contentment that immediately allows others to feel more at peace themselves. Even offering something as simple as a warm smile brings tremendous blessing to a lonely heart. Daylight work uses your innate qualities to add something good to the world.

Some parts of character that come naturally to us are not reflective of God; they are representative of our sin nature or deep wounds. Although they need to be acknowledged and addressed, they are outside the parameters of what I'd consider to be daylight work.

In John 6:1-14, a crowd of thousands was following Jesus near the Sea of Galilee. Jesus asked the disciple Philip where they could find enough food to feed everyone. I imagine Philip's eyes bugged out a bit at this question. Jesus was thinking about feeding all 5,000 of these people? *Ridiculous. Not possible. No way, Jose.* Philip replied, "It would take more than half a year's wages to buy enough bread for each one to have a bite!" (verse 7). Among the crowd of people was a boy who had five loaves of bread and two small fish. He gave them to Jesus, and the next thing we know, all the people have had a delicious dinner and there were twelve baskets of leftovers for the people to take home.

That little boy with his measly two fish and bits of bread was doing his daylight work because he was offering what he had to Jesus for the benefit of others. You don't need to be the best in your field to do your daylight work. It might not feel particularly flashy. It might even be kind of small. But when you wake up, get out of bed, and offer God to take and use what you've got, however ordinary, you're doing your daylight work.

The barista at Starbucks who always remembers your name and draws a happy face on your cup is doing her daylight work. The mom pushing two kids in the shopping cart with the squeaky wheel and planning out what's for dinner is doing her daylight work too. The musician who plays every Friday night in that dive bar where no one listens as he sings his heart out is doing his daylight work, because he is offering what he has and bringing beauty into this world, even if not everyone hears it.

It is fundamental to our Christian faith to understand that we are not saved by what we do. We are saved by faith alone, in Christ alone. Daylight work is not how we gain salvation. It's not our hall pass to heaven. It doesn't make God like us more; He already likes us. However, I admit that I more easily believe God's pleasure in me when I do my daylight work. I like seeing the way God has given me particular gifts. I enjoy knowing I have the ability to bless someone else. Feeling strong and capable is fun. And although I cannot contribute to my salvation, I like that I can contribute to God's kingdom.

To be sure, daylight work has its own set of challenges and tribulations. It contains risks and includes failures. Because daylight work is out there for all to see, our mistakes and foibles and full-on failures can be witnessed. Just because you are good at something doesn't mean you will be perfect at it. You'll have your share of face-down moments, but that's okay too. Daylight work isn't dependent upon success. Its power is in the offering itself.

If you are presently in the daylight, I cordially invite you to share your gifts with the world. We need them. You've been entrusted with talents and a unique constellation of characteristics that God has specifically placed in your hands. It's your calling to offer them back to Him by bringing them to the world, whether you are making nonfat vanilla lattes or feeding the homeless or changing diapers.

But if the sun looks to be setting soon or you are already in the depths of Midnight, the daylight work will keep. You'll still need to brush your teeth, pay the bills, and show up to your job, but you might not have as much to offer others right now. That's okay. Midnight is its own sacred time, and just as you are not to waste your gifts and talents, you are not to waste Midnight either. It will not be like your daylight work. It's not for the outside world. This is between you and God. It is an offering of a different nature. This is the place where what you thought you knew, the things you took comfort in, and the strengths you relied upon are stripped away and set on an altar to God. His holiness consumes them and you are left bare. You will discover God's pleasure in you through the broken places. You will find yourself relying fully and completely on the grace of God rather than any strengths of your own—even the ones your Creator placed in you for His glory. And the work of Midnight will begin.

Follow Me

Jesus Christ walked on the shores of the Sea of Galilee and invited disciples to follow Him. He didn't tell them what was in store. He left out details like betrayal and denial and crucifixion and potential martyrdom. He didn't coax them with exciting tales of crowds, miracles, glory, and resurrection. He simply said, "Come, follow me" (Matthew 4:19). With one call of His voice, everything changed.

Just like the first 12 disciples, each one of us has been invited to follow Jesus. And just like the disciples, He doesn't give us a lot of details about the journey ahead. Life with Christ can upend everything. It is both amazing and sometimes terribly disorienting. We get mountaintop views and valley lows. We are dazzled by bright colors and threatened by ominous gray skies. We witness new birth and the finality of death. We experience both victory and tragedy. We live with the wheat and the weeds, which sometimes are growing side by side in our own heart. We've been promised that nothing can separate us from the love of God in Christ (Romans 8:35-39), but, wow, how this life will try to do it. Tornadoes, temptations, our best days, and our worst moments will all pull at us, jeering and shouting, trying to make us lose our focus (and maybe our minds too).

Jesus is asking you to follow Him, but His path isn't for those who want predictability or a steady pace. Sometimes you will run, the wind in your hair and freedom in your feet. At other times the air around you will become thick and your pace will slow to a hesitant crawl as you enter overgrown, frightening forests. If you've been on this journey of faith for any length of time, you will have your share of heights and depths. All of it is part of following Christ. Yet just when you imagine you've walked the hardest paths, Jesus calls some of His disciples deeper still. They are asked to follow Him into places where they will lose sight of the path, themselves, and even Him altogether.

There are two times in Scripture when Jesus chose His most intimate friends—Peter, James, and John—to walk farther with Him than the other nine disciples. Once was when they witnessed the transfiguration of Jesus, when He was revealed in all of His radiant majesty and Moses and Elijah appeared with Him (Luke 9:28-36). There they saw Jesus in the fullness of His glory. On another occasion, He asked those same men to go with Him into the garden of Gethsemane. There they were exposed to the depth of His suffering: "Then Jesus went with his disciples to a place called Gethsemane, and he said to them, 'Sit here while I go over there and pray.' He took Peter and the two sons of Zebedee along with him, and he began to be sorrowful and troubled. Then he said to them, 'My soul is overwhelmed with sorrow to the point of death. Stay here and keep watch with me'" (Matthew 26:36-38).

That evening began the same way their ministry did three years before: with an invitation from Jesus to follow. Only this time, it would be into pitch blackness. For Peter, James, and John, Jesus extended an opportunity to go farther and deeper with Him, to bear witness to His personal anguish and bring Him a measure of comfort with their presence. (Which, by the way, they failed at miserably. Instead of bringing Him comfort, the disciples took a nap. #embarrassing) Jesus asked His friends to keep watch, knowing that, within hours, they would all abandon Him. Every disciple would face their own brand of terror and heartbreak, and Jesus would suffer unimaginable pain. It was the beginning of the most pivotal Midnight in history, and it was Jesus who invited them there.

The worst things don't feel like they are from a loving God, do they? Sometimes they are not. And yet God still has power over them. Which means that God can steer you away from the shadows, right? Yet He doesn't always do that. On the contrary, like the garden of Gethsemane, the Lord might ask you to follow Him *into* Midnight. And you might start asking questions like "Am I here by mistake or on purpose?" "Are these trials from God or from the enemy?"

"Do I go down this path of difficulty or do I run in the other direction?" If you are currently a resident of Midnight, these questions have occurred to you more than once. They are asked by those who God has invited into the mysterious places. It probably doesn't feel like much of an honor. Welcome to a club you never asked to join. Welcome to the nighttime of the faith journey.

This path into the dark places is sacred. God offers important, miraculous gifts wrapped in a ribbon of things you don't want. If you are part of the family of suffering, you are part of something as beautiful as it is painful. Actually it's more honest to say that you are part of something that is *becoming* as beautiful as it is painful.

Let me stop here to say that I truly, deeply hate it when people say stuff like that to me when I am hurting. When people pontificate in generalizations about my personal pain, it is often for their own comfort more than the person in pain. When they offer pat answers or quick-fix comments like "Focus on the positive!" or "Keep your chin up!" they ignore the complexity of suffering. Those remarks are also deeply shaming. They imply we haven't tried to focus on the positive, that we've done absolutely nothing to change our circumstances. Tidy, quick answers to deep suffering are usually offered by people who are either too afraid to look at their own pain or too numb to experience it. They are wounded and afraid and likely don't even know it. Their trite comments serve to distance themselves from us. They don't want to hear about our sorrow for fear of being pulled into their own.

When you are suffering, you're in your own unique place of darkness. Nothing about it feels sacred or special and you sure don't feel beautiful. Your particular journey is as complex and unique as you are, and I don't mean to start this whole thing out with words that might come across as condescending or shallow. Psalm 42:7 says, "Deep calls to deep in the roar of your waterfalls; all your waves and breakers have swept over me." I have been in the deep of Midnight often, and I have no intention of passing along platitudes or quick fixes. My words are an attempt for the deep I've experienced to call to the deep you are in so we can find one another in the mystery of this place.

You have a God who brings beauty from ashes, life from dry bones, and resurrection from the grave. He has fearfully and wonderfully created the complex nature of your soul. He is always renewing, always redeeming, always recreating. And if He does those things, then it stands to reason that your pain, your circumstance, your tears will not be left untouched or unchanged by His grace. They *will become* something beautiful. Maybe they already are beautiful. That's not a trite platitude; that's the promise of God.

The Work of Midnight

I attended a Catholic school from the third grade until I graduated high school. Yes, we wore hideous plaid skirts and the nuns were terrifying—thanks for asking. The ritual of the Catholic Mass was always a surefire way to put me to sleep. The hour-long Mass felt more like four hours, and I was sure they put something in that incense that caused overpowering drowsiness. Dorothy had no more chance of staying awake in the poppy fields of the Land of Oz than I did when Monsignor O'Sullivan led Mass in his barely understandable Irish brogue. I bet my mother would have elbowed Dorothy in the side to keep her awake too.

I could tell plenty of stories that confirm many stereotypes people have about Catholic schools. Like the time Sister Patricia picked up Dan Chaffee's entire desk over her head and threw it into the hallway in a fit of rage. Or when she threw another student's books out a second-story window for reasons that escape me. But there are a lot of aspects of growing up Catholic that have been foundational to my educational and spiritual development, and I am forever grateful. I've known the Lord's Prayer, the Nicene Creed, and all the words to "How Great Thou Art" longer than I've known my multiplication tables. I appreciate the beauty of churches built with stained glass, altars, and pews that honor the magnificence and holiness of God. In grade school, whenever we heard an ambulance pass by, we would stop whatever we were doing and bow our heads in prayer for the person who was hurt. To this day, I still pray when I hear a siren.

Another thing I remember about Catholic school was the abbreviation JMJ. We would write JMJ at the very top and center of any test or essay we were working on. It stood for Jesus, Mary, and Joseph. Being kids, we wrote it partially as a good-luck charm in hopes that Jesus Himself would coerce the teacher to overlook sloppy margins and bad spelling. (Because Jesus worries about margins, as everyone knows.) More important, writing JMJ at the top of our work was a reminder we were working unto God, which meant we were to bring our very best. It does make a girl sit up a bit straighter when she knows Jesus, Mary, *and* Joseph would also be evaluating her paper.

Colossians 3:23 says, "Whatever you do, work at it with all your heart, as working for the Lord, not for human masters." Writing JMJ at the top of our papers was our way of acknowledging we weren't simply working but we were doing our finest work in honor of the Lord.

Because Midnight work involves so much suffering, it rarely feels like your finest work. It begins when strengths end. It is grueling and ugly. Midnight work takes place in the seat of suffering. It has more snotty tissues and unbrushed hair than stained glass and pews. But it still has an altar, a chosen place where heartbreak is a fragrant offering and loss can be the start of new life.

When Jesus Christ was nailed to that cross, He cried out, "My God, my God, why have you forsaken me?" (Mark 15:34). This is the cry of Midnight. Yet His pain on the cross was when Jesus Christ did His finest work.

Midnight will invite suffering, and suffering is awful. We do not like it, we would not choose it, and when we are in the thick of it, it does not feel holy or saintly. It mostly just hurts really, really bad. This Midnight is not the Sermon on the Mount; it's the garden of Gethsemane, where we cry out in terror over all that is and all that has been lost.

I no longer write JMJ at the top of my paperwork. But I have put my life in the hands of Jesus Christ. I want my life to be glorifying to Him. I suspect you want the same thing. Our heart's desire is that we go out into this world as lights shining for Him. We long to make our work, whatever it may be, our best work. The work of Midnight will most likely never be your favorite season of life. You don't need to welcome this Midnight to discover its riches. The Lord is leading the way, and He will stay by your side. He is as comfortable here as He is in the light. He knows this place well, even the darkness is not dark to Him (Psalm 139:12). He brings sacred gifts to you in the nighttime of faith. They are luminous and mysterious and shine with His grace. Midnight is where God will do His finest work in you. It will be dark. It will be deep. And it will be radiant.

A Couple of Caveats

Most of the time, Midnight descends for a variety of reasons—known and unknown. Sometimes it begins with physical pain. Sometimes emotional. Sometimes it's a combination of experiences, thought patterns, or traumas. Midnight could be a result of those whom you have loved, who have loved you, whom you have lost, what you or someone else did or didn't do, or how you spent the first five years of life. Conversely, there might not be any direct relationship between your Midnight and your circumstances. I've had the darkness of depression land in some of the best seasons of my life. It can take you by surprise. Sometimes Midnight just *is*. I believe God always knows the exact reasons for it. But you may not. I will not minimize your struggles by trying to tie them up in a philosophical, theological, or ideological bow or by offering an arbitrary, easy explanation for all of it. However, it would be unfair to ignore two important aspects of the spiritual journey that must be acknowledged if we are to enter into the idea of exploring the experience of Midnight. Some darkness has a clear origin. I'm talking about sin and spiritual warfare.

If you are shifting in your seat now, I am too. Whenever I hear "sin" and "spiritual warfare" in the same sentence, I picture a red-faced, sweaty television preacher yelling at me and asking for money. I grew up in the eighties, when televangelism was exploding and there were scores of those guys on cable television. They all had greasy hair and plaid three-piece suits. Sin and spiritual warfare were their favorite topics to yell about. I think they wanted to scare people into heaven (or at least into donating money). So I hope you'll understand if I'm a little squeamish to talk about these topics. But we're grown-ups. If we can be brave enough to explore the darkness of Midnight, we can be brave enough to discuss what has the potential to take us there.

If the most inexplicable parts of my life were simply a result of my behavior, I would be crushed under that weight. If everything bad that happens to me were the direct result of my actions alone, I would fall into despair. It's just too much responsibility to navigate. The same goes for spiritual warfare. If "the devil made me do it," then that means he has defeated me, I have no free will, and God cannot overrule the enemy. I'm doomed. Happily, neither my sin nor Satan hold all the cards. But we must be willing to consider that both *could*—not necessarily do but could—have a part to play in our suffering, and we cannot ignore them.

Sin

In the gospel of John, the disciples see a man who has been blind since birth. They ask Jesus, "Rabbi, who sinned, this man or his parents, that he was born blind?" Jesus answered, "Neither this man nor his parents sinned, but this happened so that the works of God might be displayed in him" (9:2-3). Then Jesus healed the blind man. The disciples wanted an explanation for the man's condition. They equated suffering with sin. They liked to think that bad things (like blindness) happen to bad people and good things happen to good people. They assumed the blind man was one type of person (bad) and they were the other (good). They constructed a neat little box in which to shove the blind man so they didn't have to worry that they, too, might be struck with hardship. Jesus obliterated their box. Instead, He invited the disciples to focus on God's glory. He pulled their attention from blame to healing. And in His quiet yet intentional way, He opened up the possibility that nobody, no matter who we are or what we do, is exempt from terrible things.

It would be really convenient for me to tell you that the reason for your Midnight is because of unconfessed sin in your life. There are plenty of folks who express that sentiment. (These are the same people who have told me that if I only had more faith I would be relieved of my depression. No pressure, right?) The reasoning seems to be that if we do the right deed, pray the right prayer, and believe the right creed, we will be healed and happy. This line of thinking is understandable. We want to make sense of how we've arrived at life's awful places so we can quickly extricate ourselves from them.

On the other hand, it would be sublime to be able to tell you that the worst times of your life have nothing to do with your sin. This message would be more palatable and I bet you'd like me better. Maybe you'd give me a good review on Amazon. But I wouldn't be telling you the truth—and friends tell each other the truth.

As we saw in John 9, terrible things can happen to anyone, regardless of what they have done or not done. No wonder the insurance business is booming. A piano could fall on your head at any moment. Yet you are not exempt from ruining your own life. We are all sinners. Not one of us gets to delete that from our résumé, which means all of us will at some time or another experience the results and consequences of sin. We're in a ditch on either side. Such delightful news all around, isn't it? But hang in there with me; it gets better.

Sometimes you've marched straight into Midnight because you've made some pretty terrible decisions. You ignored the signposts, blew off the Bible, avoided sage advice, and did, as Paul says, "things which I absolutely despise" (Romans 7:15 MSG). And now, as a result, you're experiencing the consequences of your actions. Ugh. I've been there too. Like Paul, I hate when I do that. I hate that I will probably do it again in the future.

Sin—missing the mark, going astray, becoming a train wreck, whatever you want to call it—is never God's will for us. Yet sin still has the potential to bring us nearer to God. The difference between sin that motivates us to seek out God and sin that leads us away is how we react to it. One response can begin a spiritual journey; the other can result in spiritual emptiness. "If we claim to be without sin, we deceive ourselves and the truth is not in us. If we confess our sins, he is faithful and just and will forgive us our sins and purify us from all unrighteousness" (1 John 1:8-9). When we are honest with God about how we have fallen short of His will, He doesn't leave us alone—He brings us closer. Timothy Keller observed: "The gospel is this: We are more sinful and flawed in ourselves than we ever dared believe, yet at the very same time we are more loved and accepted in Jesus Christ than we ever dared hope."[5] It's both the worst and best news possible, isn't it?

In the parable of the prodigal son, Jesus tells of a son who left his father, squandered all his money, and became a cautionary tale. You know the story; it's the one of that guy in high school who flamed out quickly after graduation. Yikes. But when the prodigal son has no other alternative, he decides to go back to his dad, own up to his actions, and beg to be considered, not a family member, but a servant—anything really. Anything that would allow him to reenter the framework of his dad's property. Luke 15:20 says, "While he was still a long way off, his father saw him and was filled with compassion for him; he ran to his son, threw his arms around him and kissed him." The son limped toward home dirty, defeated, embarrassed, and ashamed. He probably looked and smelled terrible. But none of that mattered to his dad. When he saw his boy, he took off running, not stopping until he crashed into him, wrapping his arms around his boy and burying his face in his unwashed hair. His dad held him tight. He didn't care about the mess; he just wanted his child home.

When Jesus was in the garden of Gethsemane, He said, "Abba, Father, everything is possible for you. Take this cup from me. Yet not what I will, but what you will" (Mark 14:36). In His prayers, Jesus used a term for God that was different from anything anyone had used before. He called God "Abba." This Aramaic word means "father" in a familiar, informal sense. Abba is the equivalent of "Dad."[6] In His time of agony, Jesus wasn't resolutely approaching a stodgy king who demanded formality and elegance; Jesus was crying out for His *dad*. What's more, we have permission to do the same. Romans 8:15 states, "The Spirit you received does not make you slaves, so that you live in fear again; rather, the Spirit you received brought about your adoption to sonship. And by him we cry, 'Abba, Father.'"

You've got more than the omniscient God with you; you've got Abba. You have a Dad who is kind, protective, and trustworthy. He knows every hair on your head and loves you fervently. He *runs* toward you. With Abba, there is no need to pretend, ignore, defend, or deny the stuff you struggle with. He already knows. And when you bring it all to Him, you have the beautiful privilege of experiencing His grace. You will find Him running to you, arms wide open. When that happens, your relationship with your Abba only grows stronger and deeper.

A few years ago there was a person in my life who hurt me deeply. When I say hurt, I am not referring to an isolated incident. It was a steady stream of manipulation, lies, and cruelty over a long period of time. It took a tremendous toll on me. When the relationship mercifully ended and I gained some time and distance from the situation, I knew I should forgive this person. I knew it was the Christian thing to do. But I didn't want to forgive him. I didn't even *want* to want to forgive him. I hated him with a searing-hot hatred and I liked it. Hating him made me feel powerful. It made me feel good. It fueled my sense of rightness (okay, self-righteousness) and seemed to affirm his wrongness. In a relationship where I often felt bullied, the powerful experience of hating him was the best worst feeling I had had in a long time. I thought I deserved to feel that much hate and wasn't going to give it up. It didn't feel like sin. It felt like justice.

So when I felt the Lord tugging on my heart to let go of my hatred, I dug my heels in with defiance. Like a five-year-old, I crossed my arms and refused. I resented being asked to consider forgiving this person who had wounded me so deeply. I clung to my anger like a life raft and, in the process, allowed the sins of pride and self-righteousness to pull me into distant waters where I was alone with my hatred. I refused to talk about it with God. I liked talking to myself better. I liked my sin. My hardened heart made me feel strong.

Over time and in His gentle, persistent way, God kept calling me to forgiveness. Things gradually shifted. Like a glacial-speed type of gradual. I knew I needed God to take my hatred. It was too large of a load to carry by myself and it was hurting me, wearing me down and making my back (heart) sore. After a while, I slowly opened my heart enough to at least let Abba see the loathing that filled me. First, it came in the form of a prayer: "Dear God, please let him get hit by a bus. Amen."

Not exactly the prayer of Francis of Assisi. But at least I was going to God with my hardened heart instead of wrapping it in another layer of concrete. Confessing to God how much I wanted this person to be hit by a bus was the first step on the long road to forgiving him. I started to realize how scared I was to let go of my hatred, because if I let go of it, I wouldn't have any power. And then I might just feel too much pain, more than I could possibly bear. I didn't want to feel that. I decided to tell God about my fears. I told Him how much I wanted to hang on to my hatred because it was the only thing that stood between me and my heart shattering into a thousand pieces. And you know what? Walking the road of forgiveness *did* break my heart. It made me feel vulnerable and weak. I despised it. But I despised being alone with my unforgiveness even more. I wanted, no, *needed* to be within the framework of my Father's property.

The funny thing is that when we confess our sins to God, it might actually lead us into a genuine experience of Midnight. It's hard to let go of something that seems to make us feel better. Let's face it, there are some sins we really, really like. They feel useful. To let them go means we lose something, and that might mean we feel the pain of longing, powerlessness, and loss before we feel God's presence. Our hearts might break into a thousand little pieces and Midnight might descend. But if it is brought about by confession, repentance, heartbreak, and vulnerability, it will always bear fruit. He is faithful and just.

I have now forgiven that person to the best of my ability. As my ability grows, so does my forgiveness. I think that's what Jesus meant by forgiving your enemy seventy times seven. It might take that long and that many times to forgive and thereby heal one deep wound. Over and over, again and again, I forgive. Until the next time I don't feel like it, and then I go to God with that too. Sometimes I'll find myself wistfully returning to my hatred, hoping it will make me feel like it used to: powerful and brave. But it doesn't. Instead, it makes me feel lonely. I don't like being outside my Father's boundaries. I've stood too long in His grace. I've experienced Abba's steady kindness for so long, I want it more than I want to feel like I'm right. Seventy times seven. Times seven. *Times seven.*

The beauty of confession and repentance is that you can tell God about those things you desire and the loss you feel in giving them up. You can cry out and tell Him how much you miss that sin. And He draws you closer still.

At its core, sin prevents you from a deeper spiritual journey toward God. Repentance, on the other hand, leads to it. If you are holding on to sin and it is wreaking havoc on your life, you might not even be in a Midnight. You might just be experiencing the consequences and chaos of rebellion against God. If you have been holding on to your sin because you like it, believe you need it, or are afraid to let it go, you are missing out on intimacy with your Abba—the kind of intimacy that allows you to be your worst and loved at the exact same time.

John of the Cross argued that the tragedy of sin is that it actually prevents us from a Midnight.[7] He believed that the dark night of the soul is burgeoning with God's graces and that it is an experience for those who God chooses with care. He believed that in our Midnight, our Father runs to us, arms open. John of the Cross didn't want anyone to miss out on that. Neither do I.

Spiritual Warfare

Spiritual warfare is real. Satan is the accuser, and he loves to whisper half-truths and outright lies into your ears. His whisper is so soft, so cunning, so seemingly benign in tone that it's easy to mistake his voice for that of a friend, especially when you are hurting or vulnerable. Ephesians 6:12 states, "Our struggle is not against flesh and blood, but against the rulers, against the authorities, against the powers of this dark world and against the spiritual forces of evil in the heavenly realms." You must recognize that you are in a battle against things you cannot see. There is a boatload of trouble waiting to take you down when you least expect it. When you are locked in spiritual warfare, when you are being harassed by the enemy of your soul, it can feel very, very dark. But you do not need to be overwhelmed by it.*

The radiant Midnight is not the darkness of the enemy. Colossians 1:13-14 says, "He has rescued us from the dominion of darkness

---

* For practical information on spiritual warfare, its consequences, and our identity in Christ, I recommend Neil T. Anderson, *The Bondage Breaker* (Eugene, OR: Harvest House, 2000). He properly identifies the very real consequences of the spiritual realms without being histrionic or creepy.

and brought us into the kingdom of the Son he loves, in whom we have redemption, the forgiveness of sins." You are redeemed, you have been granted forgiveness, and the enemy cannot overpower you. The darkness of the enemy leads to desolation; the darkness of Midnight leads to hope.

If you've given your life in the understanding that you have been saved by the grace of God through the sacrifice of Jesus Christ, you will not be snatched away from Him. Whether your suffering is courtesy of the enemy, unforeseen events, or a result of mistakes you've made, God's got you. Jesus said, "In this world you will have trouble. But take heart! I have overcome the world" (John 16:33). The truth is that you are never fighting alone and your victory is assured.

However you've come upon this Midnight, you're here now. Feel free to get messy with laments, doubts, questions, confessions, fears, and tears. Admit to your pain, embrace your circumstances, and bring it all to the only One who can make sense of it. When you draw near to Him, He draws near to you.

David: Composer of the Songs of Midnight

David was a shepherd, musician, warrior, and king. He's described in Scripture as a man after God's own heart (1 Samuel 13:14). He trusted God deeply. He loved God fiercely. He also screwed up regularly. I mean really worst-decision-ever types of things like adultery and murder. Stuff you wouldn't want your mom to know about. Nevertheless, it all shows up in the Bible. Poor David. I'm still embarrassed by my high school hairstyles, and those only show up in old yearbooks. My bad decisions are tucked safely away within the class of '87. David's are known by billions.

But even when he was at his worst, David's faith was in the fiber of his being. Whether he was suffering as a result of his own foolishness or from someone else's cruelty, his love for God remained. His faith was rich and personal, which meant it was never neat and tidy. It was full of questions, fears, and some pretty poor choices that made it real, down-to-earth, and wincingly transparent, and it all shows up in his writing. His words reflect the unkempt maze of the human experience.

David could never be accused of keeping his feelings to himself. He holds nothing back from God, especially in the psalms he wrote. Every sob, every anguish, every heartbreak and cry of his heart are poured out in these prayers turned into songs. Many of them are all over the map. One minute David is praising the Lord. In the next he's yelling about vengeance against his enemies. And in the moment after that? He's crying out in despair. David's psalms could be described as the emotional spin cycle of Scripture. That is a great comfort to me, because I'm pretty sure I'm on the same setting. But David is always honest about his circumstances, as messy as they are. He lets all his feelings pour out from his heart to the tip of his pen.

> My heart is at anguish within me;
>   the terrors of death have fallen upon me.
> Fear and trembling come upon me,
>   and horror overwhelms me.
> And I say, "Oh that I had wings like a dove!"
>   I would fly away and be at rest;
> yes, I would wander far away;
>   I would lodge in the wilderness (Psalm 55:4-7 ESV).

I get David. You have your own story of anguish and trembling. I bet you get David too. In Psalm 55:4-7, David wasn't asking for paradise. He wasn't even asking for his pain to disappear. He just wanted a little relief. He was willing to take the snakes and man-eating lions of the wilderness rather than stay in Midnight. Maybe you'd take that deal too. A python wrapped around the neck isn't much compared to the darkness that squeezes upon the human soul.

Of the 150 psalms recorded in the Bible, at least 77 are attributed to David. In most cases, we don't know the circumstances that motivated him to write what he did. We have no idea why he is so joyful in some places and on the edge of despair in others. But we absolutely know how he was feeling when he wrote each one. Whether he is on top of the world or in the depths of despair, David makes his emotions well known. Between you and me, at times he's a bit melodramatic. For example, in Psalm 6:6, he writes, "I am worn out from my groaning. All night long I flood my bed with weeping and drench my couch with tears." Subtlety is not David's strong suit. But for those of us going through a really hard time, that's a good thing. Who needs subtlety when you feel like your guts are hanging out of your belly button?

Like the rest of Scripture, you can study the psalms to find a treasure of theological truths. But you don't need to know Hebrew to understand the meaning of most of David's songs. His vivid descriptions do the work for you. "All night long I flood my bed with weeping" paints a pretty detailed picture, doesn't it? Furthermore, because the psalms are songs, they can be approached with a nod toward artistic license. I doubt David's bed was actually flooded with his tears. But the sentiment is spot on. You get it. Your bed is probably flooded too. These songs, poems, laments, praises, and prayers can be felt more than read. Like many art forms, they explore the depth of the fragile, contradictory, and complex human heart. Through the artistry of David's words, you are invited to do more than observe; you are invited to feel, react, join in, and become part of the experience.

The Music of Midnight

The psalms reveal that David has been where you are. He was overwhelmed, anguished, and afraid. He loved God. He prayed for an end to his suffering. He complained and cried out. And because his triumph, sorrows, best moments, and worst decisions are written down in the Bible, we are given a place to go when pain renders us mute. With poetry and passion, David's intimate relationship with God birthed his psalms. In the process, he gave us the words and music to Midnight.

David brought his whole messy, unfiltered self to God. He didn't edit, judge, or soften his thoughts, feelings, and desires. Like David, trusting God in this Midnight means you will need to bring your whole self before God. It's probably going to be another great example of the emotional spin cycle. But that's okay. It just means you and David have another thing in common, besides being wildly loved by God.

In each of the following chapters, David's psalms will be our soundtrack. His anthem will become ours. His lyrics will light the path, revealing the depths of sorrow and illuminating the crevices of hope where we will find rest and healing, not on the other side, but right here, in the middle of Midnight.

Whether or not you know the reasons for this time, God is with you. He may not answer all your questions this side of heaven, but that's not what you really need. Not really. In your worst moments, in your Midnight hour, you don't need to know the exact reasons why you are there. You need to know you are not alone. You need to know there is a place to go with your pain. And there is.

Let's begin the work of Midnight.

MIDNIGHT MEDITATIONS

- What circumstances are weighing on your heart right now?

- Where can you see God working in your life and where does He remain elusive?

- Are you in the midst of a Midnight? If so, what led to it?

- How difficult is it for you to trust Him in a time of darkness and pain?

EVENING STROLL

- Find a few songs that resonate with your soul and reflect this time of Midnight. They can be any genre: country, Christian, rock, jazz, rap, or any other type of music that speaks to your soul. Make this your soundtrack. Let the music speak for you and to you.

- Find a psalm that reflects your current feelings. Read it in various translations of the Bible, such as the New International Version, the English Standard Version, The Living Bible, and The Message. Read it aloud. Make this psalm your prayer and your cry to God.

- Use David as an inspiration and write your own psalm to God. Let the words fall before Him. Trust that even if you cannot see Him or feel Him, God hears your words calling out of the darkness. And trust that He is here with you.

2

SURRENDER AND SALSA

*The sadness collapses me from the inside out, and I have to
follow the thing through until it finishes with me.*

PAT CONROY[1]

It was early in the morning and I decided to stop at a local coffee
shop to catch up on emails, read a bit, and prepare for my day
before heading into the usual busyness of the church office. It had
been a particularly grueling season in ministry, and I was stressed
out, exhausted, and emotionally drained. I also had about 243 items
on my ever-increasing to-do list. I hoped to knock a few things
off that list while surrounded by the aroma of fresh coffee and the
cheerful clatter of blenders, milk steamers, and bean grinders. By
some miracle, my favorite leather chair in my favorite corner was
available when I arrived. I set up my computer and got ready to be
productive.

I opened my email and watched as the latest dropped into
my mailbox. Some were advertisements and junk. Others were
responses to previous correspondence. Many were new from other
staff members or congregants. Every message delivered was accompanied by the familiar one-note *ding* that lets me know there is yet
another person who needs yet another thing from me.

As I stared at the list of unread emails, which were now added to the previous yet-to-be-responded-to emails from the day or maybe the week before, something stirred in me. I wasn't certain of the emotion, but it felt like dread. Every *ding* became another musical note that was building into a symphony of foreboding, like the themes from the movies *Jaws* and *Halloween* just had a baby and it was now squalling in my in-box. I took a swig of coffee for courage and (almost) pushed Open on the first email. But I couldn't do it. I took another sip. I waited for the warmth of my medium hazelnut drip (black) to take effect. Nothing.

My finger would not, could not push the button. The longer I sat sipping my coffee, the harder it became for me to move. Not just my finger but everything. My body felt like stone. The paralysis was not the "I've nabbed the only leather chair in this place so I'm going to keep it as long as I can" kind, although I've had that before. (Good chairs are hard to find!) But it was an "I'm terrified of everything" kind of paralysis. I tried to get up from the chair, but my feet wouldn't budge and my arms were lead weights.

I knew I needed to get to work. I knew I should pack up my computer and take care of all the people and plans that needed my attention. But what I knew didn't change how I was feeling. The very thought of heading into the office made my body tingle and my eyes fill with tears. I reminded myself that my responsibilities were calling me. My body only felt heavier.

I could hear the ticking of the clock; it mocked me and told me I was already late, already behind, already a failure. I tried to motivate myself with thoughts of the people at work whom I loved and who loved me. I felt nothing but an overwhelming desire to run as far away as I could. I was scared out of my mind and didn't know why.

The joy of ministry, the commitment to my coworkers, and the satisfaction of doing my job well were gone. In their place was only terror. My thoughts were scattered, incomplete, and rambling. Somehow, in the madness of my mind that was swimming (drowning) in confusion, it occurred to me that I could go home. It was the only clear thought that gave me enough strength to stand up, stumble to my car, and drive. Once home, I changed into my pajamas and lay down on the couch. I didn't turn on the television. I didn't go to sleep. I didn't call anyone. I just did nothing. It was all I could do. Nothing. That was how it went for the next few days. I think I sent out a brief email letting my coworkers know I was out sick. I vaguely remember eating from time to time. I have no idea if I brushed my teeth. Mostly, though, I did nothing.

I'd had anxiety attacks before. They were paralyzing events that made my heart race and left my body exhausted. In the middle of a panic attack, it seems like it will last forever. In reality, they've almost always ended within 20 minutes. As awful as they were, at least they were familiar territory. They had a predictable time frame with a beginning, middle, and end. This new experience, however, was a relentless onslaught of anxiety and fear that would not abate.

After several days of hemming and hawing, out of total desperation, I went to my physician. He prescribed some medication that helped stop the cycle of panic and exhaustion. After a few days my mind felt clearer and my heart didn't race anymore. But I was still exhausted. It felt like I had been running downhill and couldn't stop until I hit a wall face-first. Bam! Just like that, I was down for the count. I was bloodied, bruised, and disoriented. Getting up again took a while.

Returning to work after two weeks away was grueling. I no longer had the energy that allowed me to juggle a myriad of responsibilities and pressures. The spigot of ideas and creativity that usually flowed freely from my mind became a drip. Every day felt laborious. No matter how hard I tried, I could not return to my former self.

It's not like I was comatose or that my coworkers saw a drastic change in me. I wasn't walking around with a rain cloud over my head and a box of tissues in my hand. I didn't fall asleep at my desk (although I wanted to). I was social, engaged, and accomplished my day-to-day tasks. But I was different. That day in the coffee shop, I ran face-first into my own limitations. They left me bruised and broken, and I didn't quite know what to do with myself.

Were there circumstances in my life that led to this? Was there a cause behind all of it? Yes and no. Yes, there were difficult things going on, but no, there was nothing immediate that caused the shift I experienced that day. I mean, I had three sips of coffee and simply opened my laptop. How hard could the morning have been?

Discovering Your Limitations

When we run headlong into our limitations, it's like moving from a four-bedroom home to a studio apartment. At each turn, there's a wall. There's not as much room to spread out, to move, to live. It's not like there's *no* home, but it's certainly more constrained than it was. Because the home is now smaller, all the furniture and possessions that once coordinated perfectly in the previous place now crowd in and prevent free, unhindered movement. To live well within these new walls, we must make the difficult choice to let go of the things that no longer fit. This is not easy, because many of those things worked so well for so very long. They were beautiful and had significant meaning. It's not that they are broken or ruined or useless, but they just don't fit anymore. To find beauty in the limitations of this new living space, no matter what circumstance brought it about, we must surrender the things that no longer belong.

Sometimes surrender happens voluntarily; we give up those things that no longer fit with intentionality (or at the very least resignation). Sometimes control is ripped out of our hands so quickly that surrender is not a choice at all. Instead of being able to let go slowly, everything familiar and beautiful is abruptly taken in one swift motion.

When Midnight descends, life is different. In order for Midnight to do its work, it needs to be. If you find yourself in more limited quarters, you are in the right place. If you are not able to accomplish as much as you used to, that is okay, because you are in Midnight. You might not be as patient, generous, or creative as you were before. The world gets smaller. Your abilities get smaller. It will feel wrong, but it won't be wrong.

Whether or not you want to do more, Midnight is the time when you cannot do more. If you kick against your limitations in the belief that they are barriers preventing you from being your best, you will miss out on what surrender has to offer. It doesn't feel heroic or inspiring to surrender. It might not even feel like the Christian thing to do.

Most of us love underdog stories. We read books and watch movies about those who overcome the odds. In the Christian tradition, there are amazing stories of faithful believers who do incredibly brave, inspiring things in the name of the gospel. They accomplish great things and give the glory to God. As a result, these stories remind us that anything is possible. They encourage us to be bold, to keep fighting, to believe in God and in ourselves.

When you run up against your limitations, it might be very tempting to fight back and to stay strong, like the protagonist in an underdog movie. It's an option, but I don't think it will serve you well in this sacred season of surrender. Your limitations are not barriers preventing you from success or strength. Perhaps your limitations are protecting you from being too busy, too independent, and too competent for your own good. You will need to trust that God is doing some of His best work even when it feels like you are at your worst.

In *Let Your Life Speak*, Parker Palmer wrote, "Each of us arrives here with a nature, which means both limits and potentials. We can learn as much about our nature by running into our limits as by experiencing our potentials."[2] This "running into our limits" is a humbling process. It doesn't always sit well with your ego, and it doesn't always sit well with others. It requires you to say no often, and you'll likely need to let opportunities pass. In this season, you will probably disappoint people. Your pride may get bruised because people might assume things about you that are not true. There is a cost associated with Midnight.

The work of Midnight requires vulnerability and will ask you to set aside the things that make you feel strong. It will invite humility far more than competency. The work of Midnight is to lay bare your utter dependency on God for absolutely everything. He becomes your one and only portion. When your body is too heavy to lift, when your mind slows to a crawl, and when the strengths you once relied on elude you, Abba is inviting you to open the gift of surrender.

Like moving from a large house to a small apartment, you must examine your life and decide what no longer belongs. You might need to set certain things aside for a while, not because those things are useless, but simply because the work of Midnight requires a smaller space. If you are still passionate about them when dawn breaks, you can reincorporate them back into your life. For now, though, it's time to simplify. You can trust that if God has placed talents and abilities in you, He cherishes them even more than you do. He will guard them and keep them safe while you traverse this Midnight hour.

Jesus Christ, on the last night of His life, was tormented by fear and foreboding. His triumphal entry, the crowds of admirers, even His closest friends were stripped away. The people who had shouted "Hosanna!" the week before would soon be shouting "Cru-cify Him!" And He would enter into a pain we can only imagine. His strengths—the things that remained true to who Jesus was, His power to make miracles, His might to call angels to His aide, His glory that invited Moses and Elijah to appear by His side—were all set aside. It's not that He didn't have access to them. The essence of Jesus never left Him. But this was His Midnight, and the work of Midnight requires surrender more than strength.

The essence of who you are will not be lost in this season. But your abilities might be diminished. You will not be able to do all you want to do. You may not be able to juggle daily responsibilities, the normal interruptions life brings, *and* new projects simultane-ously. You might need to do them just a bit at a time or let some of them go altogether. When you are in Midnight, when you have set aside your strengths (or had them ripped out of your hands), sur-render is the only dish on the menu. You might as well grab a fork and dig in.

Detour

> I cry aloud to the LORD,
>> I lift up my voice to the LORD for mercy.
> I pour out before him my complaint,
>> before him I tell my trouble.
> When my spirit grows faint within me,
>> it is you who watch over my way (Psalm 142:1-3).

David knew God. David was sure of God. And God was sure of David. When David was just a boy, the Lord declared that David would be the next king of Israel (1 Samuel 16:1-13). At the time of this announcement, David had not done anything remotely king-like to deserve this honor. David was working for his dad, herd-ing sheep. It's not like he was already making weapons or figuring out war strategies. His experience did not indicate any greatness to come. Nevertheless, David believed in God's calling (1 Samuel 16:12). From the day God anointed him, his destiny was set. David knew that he *knew* that he would be king.

Over the next few years he acquired the experience he lacked when he was younger. I suspect that his assured calling gave him great confidence. He was going to be king! God was on his side! He was bold and daring and faithful. He killed a giant with a slingshot. He served in the courts of King Saul. He won a lot of wars on Saul's behalf. With every victory, the people's love for David increased. He even married Saul's daughter. David now had experience, a royal wife, victories in battle, and the support of Israel. With God's anointing in place, his path looked like a straight shot to the throne. Except it wasn't.

"When Saul saw how successful he was, he was afraid of him" (1 Samuel 18:15). David was prophesied to be the next king, but Saul initially wasn't too worried. After all, David was just some kid. As David grew and accomplished more and more, Saul started to feel unsettled. He had long ago stopped obeying the Lord. Moreover, it looked like David would indeed be king. Saul knew it. The people knew it. So Saul decided to do something about it.

Kings generally don't like being upstaged. And they definitely don't like scuttlebutt about a new king while they're still on the throne. Saul decided to kill David, and David had to run for his life. Instead of the grandiosity of a palace, the fervor of the battlefield, or even the expanse of a shepherd's field, the next decade or so of David's life was spent hiding in small, dark caves and in the tangle of wilderness (1 Samuel 23:14). He was pursued, threatened, and feared for his life.

At Midnight a lot of things fall apart. Not just you. Your dreams and expectations take a big hit too. Perhaps you've been on a good path. Things have been steady. Maybe you, like David, are sure of your calling in life, and yet here you are, in the cave of Midnight, off the path you were sure was set out for your life. All that was certain gets tangled up and left in the brambles of the wilderness. It feels very, very wrong. It feels like a detour. Like a mistake. How can God be glorified when defeat is surrounding you on all sides?

When Saul decided to kill him, David had only known victory. He knew all about the spoils of war and the cheers of the people. He knew strategy. He knew how to conquer. He knew boldness and strength. But he did not know how to surrender. Until the darkness of the caves surrounded him, David never had to.

Part of Midnight is surrendering what you think should happen in your life. Maybe you thought you would be healed of your wounds by now. Maybe you felt destined for wide-open spaces and instead you're now living in a one-bedroom apartment with a leaky kitchen sink. Perhaps it feels a lot like a cave. Maybe you have felt strong and capable, but now all of that is slipping away. Defeat feels imminent. And in the middle of the mess, I'm discussing surrender? What a punch in the gut. I'm so sorry. If I could avoid suggesting it, I would. But since Midnight is for those whom Abba invites into a deeper, stronger, more mysterious faith, then surrender plays too important a role to ignore.

God's anointing of David took place before everything hit the fan. David was chosen before he was even cut out to be king. His success in the heat of battle might have convinced him that he was indeed destined for greatness. But it was his time in the caves that taught him where his greatness would come from. In the damp darkness of a cave, David ran into his limits. He couldn't control Saul and he couldn't control God. His calling as king was overshadowed by the reality of the cave. David had to let go of his expectations of himself as much as God. He had to surrender the path he thought he was going to take and face the unplanned, untamed wilderness.

To be clear, letting go is not the same as giving up. Giving up means that all hope is lost and you are sunk. Giving up means that victory is not possible. Giving up means God is finished and there is nothing left for you. On the other hand, letting go is loosening your grip. It's opening your hands and allowing your plans to fall away. It's the decision to stop holding on to what might need to be released. Just as God had plans for David, He has plans for you. You are not finished. Midnight is no time to give up. But it *is* time to let go.

Even in the darkness of the cave, when everything pointed to his sure defeat, David never gave up. He knew God had a path even when he couldn't see it. He knew the cave would not be his final resting place. But he had to let go of his expectations of how he would arrive in the wide open places. He had to let go of what he imagined his life to be. The light of his path evaporated, and the only step he knew to take was the next one. He surrendered his strength, his plans, and the shouts of the crowd to God. He leaned into the weakness of the unknown.

During his time on the run, David had more than one opportunity to kill Saul. At one point Saul walked into the very cave where David was hiding (1 Samuel 24:3-4). David's men were there too, telling him this was the moment to strike, this was the day God's anointing would be realized. It would have made perfect sense for David to kill Saul in that moment of opportunity. With the swing of his sword, David could have cut through Midnight altogether. He could have killed Saul and walked into the bright light of victory. He could have put his life back on the track he imagined for himself. But David knew that it was not his calling to get rid of Saul. That was God's territory. In obedience and trust, David surrendered to God's will and didn't raise a hand against the man who was fervently seeking to destroy him. David remained quiet in the darkness of the cave, resolved to wait for God's timing. Saul walked away intact. And David's Midnight lasted longer because of it.

It seemed like the plans of God took David further away from the life promised to him. But the point of Midnight is not simply to get out of it. It's to trust God in it. It is there to teach us things we cannot learn on the paved roads of our own plans. Faith is discovered in the savage brush of the wilderness. It will scratch your legs and make you tromp through muck and mire. You will wonder where it is all leading. But God knows this wilderness. Keep going. One agonizing step at a time. Remember Psalm 142:3, where David cries to God, "When my spirit grows faint within me, it is you who watch over my way." In other words, when it all seems lost, I'll surrender my expectations to Your path, God. I'll leave the paved roads of my own plans behind and follow You into the uncharted darkness of the caves. I will trust Your way. But would You hurry up? I'm dying here.

This Isn't About Them—It's About Him

Sometimes Midnight is ushered in by a conglomeration of situations that add up to untenable pain. Death, job loss, depression, divorce, or financial troubles are not about one individual person or relationship; they are often about uncontrollable circumstances. Maybe it's not anyone's fault. It just happened. At other times, Midnight can fall swiftly with one phone call, one test result, one conversation.

Maybe Midnight has descended as the result of deep wounds inflicted by someone else. The deepest pain you can experience is at the hands of someone you loved who should have loved you back. Instead of cherishing and protecting it, someone took the softest part of your heart and eviscerated it. Maybe the wounds have come in the form of a thousand small cuts. Because the damage was incremental, you didn't even know you were bleeding until it was almost too late. Maybe it's only now, as Midnight descends, that you realize the enormity of the wounds endured at the hands of someone you trusted. Sometimes you are so close to a person, you never suspect they are the source of your tremendous pain. A little distance and time are needed before it dawns on you that a person you've loved has slowly been poisoning you. When you realize something like that, it's time to let go.

In war, surrender is a bad thing. It means defeat. It means being the loser. At best, defeat produces a participation award. At its worst, it means death. Remember all those movies set in medieval times where men fight to the death while large crowds watch and cheer and eat turkey legs? There are no participation awards at those games, just a guy who sweeps dirt over the blood of the last dead loser.

The betrayal, the heartlessness, the sheer cruelty that can be inflicted upon you by another human being is staggering. What is worse than that? Watching that same person skip off into the sunset like nothing really terrible happened. Comparing their life to your pain can serve as a barometer for how defeated you believe yourself to be. The better they seem, the worse you feel. The worse you feel, the more it looks like they've won and you've lost. There's a guy in the ring throwing dirt over your spilled blood, and everyone else is sitting back, eating their turkey legs, having a grand old time.

So when you consider the act of surrendering, it's no wonder it seems like a victory for your enemies and your defeat. But Midnight isn't about your enemies, because you are not surrendering to them. You are not surrendering to your circumstances. You are not surrendering to depression, divorce, grief, betrayal, cancer, or loneliness. You are not turning yourself over to any enemy. David never surrendered to Saul, even when he spared his life. Like David, you are surrendering to God alone.

The Weight of Tacos

A few years ago my family and I went on a mission trip with our church to Ensenada, Mexico. We spent three days building a home for a family who had been living in a leaking shack made of discarded wooden pallets. They had a small area outside that they used to cook all their meals over a fire they kept constantly kindled. They owned only a few pots and pans. This quiet young couple had three small children who never experienced the simplicity of a warm bath or running water. Our church group was ready to help.

I cannot imagine what this humble family must have thought when a group of 25 men, women, and children descended on them. We were loud, jovial, and determined to build a structure that would protect them from the elements and give them a measure of dignity. Only a few in our group spoke Spanish, but that didn't stop the rest of us from trying. I enthusiastically engaged the family by bobbing my head up and down, grinning profusely, and repeating wildly the only word I remembered from two years of high school Spanish class: "Casa! Casa!" They were probably terrified of me. I wouldn't blame them.

Day two of the trip was the longest. From sunup to sundown, we were hammering, drywalling, spackling, and roofing. We brought our own lunches and planned to eat dinner back at the dormitories where we were staying. Just as the sun was setting and we were preparing to finish for the day, the mother and father came over to us with paper plates. They invited us to eat with them. We'd been so busy working, we never noticed they had been cooking a feast. There, in every dish, pot, and pan they owned, were the fixings for fish tacos. Lettuce, sour cream, handmade tortillas, and freshly caught fish were spread out before us in a banquet. I've never seen anything so beautiful. In the midst of extreme poverty, we were offered abundance.

They made enough food to feed all of us. I cannot imagine how much this must have cost them. I was stunned and incredibly uncomfortable. I cannot think of any other way to say it: I was horrified. It panicked me that this impoverished family would go out of their way to do something so extravagant for us. We came to serve *them,* not the other way around. I didn't want to eat. It felt like stealing. But the family was insistent, and for fear of offending them, I grabbed a plate. I proceeded to bite into the best fish tacos I've ever had. Ever. And trust me, I've eaten my share of tacos through the years. These were outstanding. Tears welled up in my eyes as I ate, not only because of the flavor, but because I was overcome with emotion. This family gave out of their poverty. In one night we dined on what they probably ate in a month. They offered to us what they did not have for themselves. Are there words for such an act of kindness?

To this day I have a hard time putting my finger on the complexity of feelings I experienced that night (and still experience when I think of it). Those tacos terrified and embarrassed me. I felt completely out of control. I was utterly helpless in the face of this family's generosity. I felt vulnerable. As if I were naked. I wanted to cry, to run, to do anything but eat those fish tacos, because I knew (or didn't know, which was worse) what it cost them. I wanted to express gratitude to them without receiving anything, but there wasn't a way to do that. Is this what being humbled feels like? I don't know. But in that moment, my only choice was to pick up a plate and enjoy the magnificence of what I'd been offered.

Surrendering to God is like eating those tacos. (I'm confident the great theologians of our time have never compared surrendering

to God to tacos, but stick with me here.) I'm sure there are people who have surrendered with grace and aplomb. But the rest of
us? Especially those of us experiencing a disorienting Midnight?
We're tempted to cry, run, or do anything that makes us feel less
vulnerable.

God's grace is freely given, but as Dietrich Bonhoeffer said, it
is not cheap.[3] The grace you're given through Christ is priceless. It
cost Him everything. Jesus went through torture, humiliation, and
unimaginable agony on our behalf. He didn't deserve any of it. The
horror of the crucifixion and all that it means can reduce us to utter
helplessness in the face of His generosity.

God's love has weight to it. It has substance. It has shape and
form and does not go unnoticed by those who experience it. Because
it is real, it changes people. The love of God has the capacity to shape
and affect us and create whole new chapters in our life story. It can
flood our empty spaces and bandage our wounds. Because of His
love, we have been made worthy of His unending mercy. The weight
of God's love settles down inside of us, and we are different because
of it.

We don't always want to feel that weight. Sometimes it overwhelms us to be loved so completely, so patiently, so personally.
It makes us aware of how utterly vulnerable we are. We might
feel naked in the light of His love. We have neither earned it nor
deserved it, which creates that niggling thought inside our brains
that because we haven't done anything to get it, there is nothing we
can do to keep it.

Depending on God can be terrifying. You might be tempted to
push your vulnerability away and turn your face from it. Sometimes
I find myself trying to think of another way I can be grateful without needing Him so completely. So far I haven't come up with anything. At other times I'm aware of just how nasty my thoughts can

be and how un-Christlike I am. I feel ashamed that I so easily fail at being the person I want to be. But even then, it's not His judgment I fear most; it's His love. Compassion that big frightens me.

The Gift of Surrender

> I used to think the spiritual life was mostly about finding and using our gifts for God's glory—my utmost for his highest. More and more, I think it is not this, not first, not most. At root, the spiritual life consists in choosing the way of littleness.
>
> —MARK BUCHANAN[4]

Have you ever been in a situation where you might cry at a moment's notice and you really don't want to? The tears are sitting right there, ready to spring forth at the slightest word or deed. Sure, in those moments, even the slightest unkind word can make me bawl like a baby. But what do I dread even more than an unkind word when I am most vulnerable? Love.

It is my dear friends who can really ruin me when I am hurting. When I am in public and on the verge of tears, the last thing I want is for a friend to ask me how I am. If I look into the eyes of one who really knows and loves me, the tears will be unleashed and I will ugly cry in two seconds flat. And if I'm in line at the grocery store, I don't want to ugly cry. So in situations like that, I avoid my friends. I will try to breeze past them in the frozen food aisle. If they insist on talking to me, I tell them, "Don't be nice to me. Don't ask me anything. Don't say anything kind to me." I know I won't be able to handle experiencing that amount of love when I do not have the strength to accept it with dignity. And I like dignity. I cling to it like the last doughnut at church on a Sunday morning. But that is not always good for me. (Neither is the doughnut, for that matter.)

Anthony Bozza of *Rolling Stone* magazine did an interview with U2 singer Bono in 2001. Bono described the experience of being with his dying father in his last days:

> Me…I was sleeping beside him. I'd get back home after gigs we were doing in Europe and England and have a pint of Guinness and a chaser to steady my nerves, then I'd go into the hospital and I'd sleep beside him, you know, because I didn't want him to be alone at night…He's a tough guy, really, just tough…I had a bit of an epiphany about it all. My prayer for him was that he would keep his dignity. He had a lot of front. But he didn't get to keep his dignity. Cancer is very cruel in the way that it kills you so slowly. But I, you know, I sat there. I drew him. I held his hand. I did things that he would never let me do. He was trapped…But I thought that maybe dignity is not such a big deal. I had dignity up there with righteousness, something you'd aspire to. But the two most important events of your life—being born and dying—are very messy. Very messy. Giving birth is very messy for mother and child…
>
> Maybe humility is the eye of the needle that we all have to pass through.[5]

Bono had the chance to hold his father's hand because dignity and pride had been stripped way. Lying in that hospital bed, his dad was vulnerable to his illness, to his limitations, to his circumstance. But that wasn't all. Those same things allowed him to be vulnerable to a love and comfort unavailable to (or rather unneeded) by him at his strongest. And a son got to hold his father's hand.

The gift of surrender is to experience the full weight of God's love without your own competence getting in the way. In the light of the magnificence of His love and grace, your strengths will only serve as hindrances. Whatever stake is buried deep in your flesh, it is a conduit to a deeper power than anything you can produce on your own. This surrender, this laying down of yourself and all you rely on apart from God, might feel like darkness descending. There is nothing so disintegrating as coming face-to-face with your own weakness. Yet there is nothing so comforting as discovering His strength.

> I cry to you, LORD;
>> I say, "You are my refuge,
>> my portion in the land of the living."
> Listen to my cry,
>> for I am in desperate need;
> rescue me from those who pursue me,
>> for they are too strong for me (Psalm 142:5-6).

Spoiler alert: David eventually became king. His time in the wilderness didn't last forever, though there were days that probably felt like it. Every scrape, every sleepless night, every tangled brush and damp cave in the middle of nowhere taught David surrender. Midnight taught him to trust in his God more than in what he could see or understand. It highlighted his limitations so he could surrender to the unlimited God. Midnight stripped away his ideas of how his life should go and whittled down his resources to one: his Lord. His refuge and portion in the land of the living. Midnight strengthened David in ways that even the most glorious battlefield victories could not. It took away what was no longer necessary and taught David that the only portion he really needed was God. Midnight was as much a part of David's destiny as was his royalty.

It's been a few years since that day in the coffee shop. I still reflect on it, though. Running into the wall of my limitations was painful and demoralizing. Letting go of abilities I relied on to make me feel healthy and strong was humbling. Realizing how little control I had over my own mind and body was terrifying. All of it made me feel vulnerable and naked.

I have never returned to my same ability to juggle so many things. I'm okay with that now. My life is quieter, softer, and less chaotic. I don't work at a church anymore. Sometimes I miss the pace and the excitement of keeping so many balls in the air. It was fun to do so much for so long. I certainly miss the people and the camaraderie of the staff. Those things were good and important for that season, and I don't regret a minute of it. I'm just not in that season anymore.

The work of Midnight will quiet the soul. It will teach us how to embrace limitations and trust the strength of God's love rather than our own abilities. We can slowly learn to let go. God produces strength through weakness and value through poverty. In His hands, surrender is the strongest thing you can do. The apostle Paul wrote: "God chose what is foolish in the world to shame the wise; God chose what is weak in the world to shame the strong; God chose what is low and despised in the world, even things that are not, to bring to nothing things that are, so that no human being might boast in the presence of God" (1 Corinthians 1:27-29 ESV). Coming to the end of yourself and feeling low or foolish for doing it is the beginning of something new.

In the midst of your poverty of strength, God is offering you the gift of surrender. Like when I was offered those tacos in Mexico, maybe you're so vulnerable at the moment that you feel trapped, like you have no choice but to take it. It's embarrassing, scary, and humbling. It feels wild and untamed. It is the road less traveled. It is covered with brush and bramble and there are dark caves and black nights. But you are safe with Him. Take what He is offering. Follow this unwieldy path. You are not giving up. By embracing your limitations and surrendering your will to Him alone, you are learning to live in His unlimited, unending, unfathomable grace.

MOONLIGHT MEDITATIONS

- What strengths and abilities have you relied upon that are not with you in this time?

- What limitations are you discovering in your Midnight?

- How might surrender be a gift even when it feels like defeat?

- In the powerful gaze of the One who loves you, have you responded, "Don't be nice to me" because you didn't want to feel naked and vulnerable? Have you chosen dignity over dependency and inadvertently missed this gift of a dark place?

EVENING STROLL

- Write down each of your strengths—the ones that you know with certainty are from God—on index cards (one strength per card). If you are not sure what they are, ask a close friend. They'll tell you in a heartbeat. Now place the cards in an envelope. Seal the envelope and write on the front "To be opened in daylight" to remind yourself that some of your strengths are not gone, just sealed away for a bit and that daylight will come again.

3

NO THING LEFT

Messiness is the workshop of authentic spirituality, the greenhouse of faith, the place where the real Jesus meets the real us.

Michael Yaconelli[1]

Tackling the topic of suffering this early in the book might not be the best way to keep you reading into chapter 4. You might ask, "If this is just the beginning, then where do we go from here? What other gifts in dark places are there? Root canals? Snake bites? Enduring endless episodes of *Gilligan's Island*?" All fair questions. But I'm hoping you will hang in there with me. I promise there is no chapter about bamboo shoots and fingernails.

But if Midnight is surrounding you right now, you're already suffering. And your suffering is too important to me and certainly too important to God to wait until halfway through this book to address it just so I can ease you into this whole awful, beautiful, messy topic.

In my finer moments I see the value of suffering. I can appreciate the growth and lessons learned from the painful things in life, like a job that never quite works out or the heartbreak of a first romance. In Romans 8:28, Paul said, "We know that in all things God works for the good of those who love him, who have been called according to his purpose." I believe the truth in Romans 8:28, but when I am overwhelmed with sorrow and pain, this verse brings little comfort. I highly recommend *not* whipping it out to a friend who's in the throes of suffering. There are some things that happen in this life-time that will never, ever make complete sense.

My friend Kay's son was killed in Afghanistan. My friend Mary Jo experienced the death of her son three hours after he was born. My brother-in-law committed suicide. To try to explain why God allows what He does in a particular situation is hubris; it cheap-ens someone else's suffering and it cheapens God to think we can know every reason for all the awful things that happen in this world. We can know with certainty, however, through our claustrophobic, cruel waves of grief, God saves every tear we shed (Psalm 56:8). We can know there is not one event in our life that is wasted or worth-less to God. That doesn't mean we can explain it now or even that it's appropriate to try. When Midnight has descended and every-thing has stopped making sense, and you think you might die of overwhelming sadness, it really doesn't matter at that moment why you are suffering. You only want it to stop. Right now.

Make It Go Away

I was 13 when I first experienced what I now know was depres-sion. Back then it progressed like slow-growing moss on a tree; incrementally moving and settling into all the carved-out places in my heart. By my junior year in high school, it covered almost all of me. I wanted it to stop. Depression feels like being locked in a small room without doors or windows. No matter how much I wanted out, no matter how much I tried, I could not escape.

Back then my resources to cope were limited and unhealthy. I would stick pins in my arms or drag thumbtacks across my thighs until I drew blood. When I felt the physical pain of my actions, I experienced temporary relief from the gnawing that seemed to be taking over my insides. When I got older, I would drink until I passed out or smoke pot. I'm not proud of any of this. But to this day it makes perfect sense to me why I did those things. The desire to escape suffering makes us desperate and unreasonable, because we just want it to *stop*. If we are in a large amount of pain, our first reaction is to make it stop in the quickest, but not necessarily the healthiest, way possible.

Your body was built for self-protection. You instinctively move your hand away from a hot flame and avoid eating apples if you have a toothache. Your natural aversion to pain makes you avoid it as much as possible. But pain usually points to something that needs attending to, and in the desire to remove the pain as quickly as possible, your self-protective reactions can prevent you from the true healing for which your soul longs.

My son, Cole, was ten years old when I got the bright idea to watch the movie *End of the Spear* with him. It's based on the true story of Jim and Elisabeth Elliot and their friends who moved to Ecuador with the desire to share Jesus Christ with the tribal people who lived in these remote jungles. It's an extraordinary story of bravery, faith, and forgiveness, and I thought my son would love it.

Most parents have had those glorious moments when they realize too late they've made a grave misstep in their decision making. Watching this movie with Cole was one of those moments. Cole was completely immersed in the movie by the time the likable, affable Jim Elliot and his friends were brutally murdered by the men they desired to help. It was a violent, bloody scene. I had utterly forgotten the story of Jim Elliot is one of unmitigated horror as much as it is about faith. Cole hid his eyes and cried, "Mom, turn it off! Turn it off! I can't watch it anymore! It's too awful!"

Everything in me wanted to shut off the television right then and there. Cole's anguish was heartbreaking. I regretted ever renting the movie and realized I'd underestimated the power of the story and the depth of my son's sensitivity. I'd made a big, fat mistake. But there was no going back. Here we were. And the question remained: What should I do next? After pausing the movie and holding Cole for a few minutes, I decided we needed to watch the rest of the movie. Cole was emphatically not in favor of this; he wanted to leave. I told him he was to stay put. In short, I made the choice to help Cole move into his suffering instead of removing it.

Henri Nouwen wrote, "Our efforts to disconnect ourselves from our own suffering end up disconnecting our suffering from God's suffering for us. The way out of our loss and hurt is in and through."[2] Cole needed to see the rest of the story, because the way out of his hurt was in and through it. He needed to watch the grief and sadness that Elisabeth Elliot and her child experienced as a result of Jim's awful death. Only by seeing the horror of the murder and the pain it caused could Cole then understand the enormity of the Elliot family's decision to return to Ecuador a year later and share the gospel with the same people who had murdered Jim. If we turned off the movie and walked away, Cole would not witness the grace, the forgiveness, and the incredible faith of the Elliot family. Instead, he would have been left with images of the bloodied bodies lying at the edge of a river.

When you move into your pain instead of away from it, you allow suffering to do its work. If you cut short the process, you will not be able to experience the healing work that Midnight has to offer. You will claw and scratch and grope your way through this awful darkness of anguish and stay focused on getting out. In the process, you will miss the sacred gifts waiting for you here in the dark places. Suffering goes against your innate sense of self-protection, and that doesn't feel good. But it is necessary.

Judge, Jury, and Executioner

When my kitchen counters are clean, a tiny part of me feels like a better Christian. I know it's not theologically accurate, but if I can put a piece of paper on my countertop without its landing in a glob of jelly, I feel good about myself. Even better, I feel more likable to God. When I feel strong, optimistic, and good, I feel more like the person I want to be for my family, myself, and for God.

When I'm depressed and tired, when my feelings are hurt, when my kitchen counter is sticky, I don't like myself very much. When I'm struggling, I don't feel patient or nice, let alone feel like a good Christian. When I have anxiety and am afraid to get out of bed or don't want to be around people, I suspect God is irritated. In my rational mind, I know nothing can separate me from God's love. But I'm not always rational. When I feel terrible, I feel bad.

It starts when we are little: "Be a good girl, and I will get you some ice cream." "If you're a bad boy, no ice cream for you!" Good means we behave nicely and are pleasant and compliant. Bad means we are negative and bothersome. Good means we get ice cream with sprinkles on it. Bad means no ice cream and definitely no sprinkles.

The problem is that we place value judgments like these on our suffering. Because suffering feels so bad, it's easy to believe *we* are bad. Or we think that we are not "suffering well" because we feel like a mess. It feels like we've done something wrong because our feelings are negative, bothersome, and sour. But *feeling* bad and *being* bad are not the same thing.

Pain is not morally right or wrong. It just is. But that's easy to forget. When we've been sad for a while, when we've tried to look on the bright side and it's still dark, we might become our own cruel judge and jury. In our shame we condemn what we cannot control: our suffering. We just know that if we feel this bad for this long, there is something terribly wrong with us. We are certain we are not supposed to hurt this much, cry this hard, or feel this awful. We are sure other people don't feel the same way. We are positive other Christians don't struggle this much. We are ashamed of our weakness, our brokenness, and our inability to be stronger and braver than we are. When we feel this bad, we are sure God thinks we are bad. We just know, deep in our soul, that we are a disappointment to God.

The French philosopher Voltaire is believed to have said, "If God created us in His own image, we have more than reciprocated."[3] Most of us put words in the mouth of God more times than we care to admit. It's not that anyone intends to. It's just that when we are in the throes of suffering, we forget we do not see our life as God does. We do not see ourselves as God does. We definitely don't see our suffering as God does.

The suffering of Midnight can be confusing and disorienting. It's easy to let your mind run wild and get jumpy. You need something more reliable than your own thoughts and feelings when you are hurting. Actually, you need that all the time, but especially when you're hurting. So it's convenient that God chose to reveal His thoughts in Scripture. You need them in black and white so you can read them over and over and let them penetrate your wounded heart. You need to read the truth so you can stop listening to the lies of your own thoughts. "'For my thoughts are not your thoughts, neither are your ways my ways,' declares the LORD. 'As the heavens are higher than the earth, so are my ways higher than your ways and my thoughts than your thoughts'" (Isaiah 55:8-9).

Your feelings are tremendously important to God. But they are not necessarily a reflection of God. Your feelings are real and they matter, but they are not where you find truth. God is the creator and keeper of what is true. The truth of His Word outweighs what feels true. No matter how harshly you judge your plight, how horrible you feel, or how sticky your kitchen counters are, you have a God of compassion and comfort. His Word is truer than feelings about yourself that surge, swirl, and move. He is a safe, consistent place to go with your pain: "A bruised reed he will not break, and a faintly burning wick he will not quench" (Isaiah 42:3 ESV). He invites you to cast all of your fear and pain onto His kind, broad shoulders: "Let [the Lord] have all your worries and cares, for he is always thinking about you and watching everything that concerns you" (1 Peter 5:7 TLB). He is not immune to the suffering of His children. He sees the pain of His people. Jesus was moved by the crowds of people who surrounded Him: "When he saw the crowds, he had compassion for them, because they were harassed and helpless, like sheep without a shepherd" (Matthew 9:36). He is not waiting for you to come to Him so He can lecture or shame you. He wants good things for you. God offers rest for your weary soul: "Come to me, all who labor and are heavy laden, and I will give you rest. Take my yoke upon you, and learn from me, for I am gentle and lowly in heart, and you will find rest for your souls. For my yoke is easy, and my burden is light" (Matthew 11:28-30 ESV). The significance of your feelings never overrides the infallibility of God's truth.

Have you circumvented the love and grace God has to offer by categorizing feelings you don't like as bad? By deciding you know the truth about the morality or immorality of your suffering, you are cutting off the invitation that God, the keeper of real truth, is holding out to you. The judgment of your most loathsome feelings is a cruel adversary of grace. It is not your job to judge the feelings you have. It is your job to steward them well by confessing them, respecting them, and by allowing Abba to see them in all their undeveloped, untethered, undone messiness. Anything less will harm your spirit and prevent you from living as you truly are: loved beyond measure, accepted without mitigation, absolutely seen, known, and understood in your suffering.

Midnight takes place in the dark. It is a time to slow down and sit a while. You will not be able to see clearly, which means you're going to need to hold off judging where you are and what it means. Darkness, like pain, is not moral or immoral. It just is.

Grasping Water

Maybe acknowledging and confessing our feelings scares us because we're afraid to experience their raw, unhinged power. Sometimes we are afraid to feel the full weight of our sorrow, pain, and sadness because, if we do, we might be swallowed whole by them. So we try to keep them at bay, talking ourselves out of pain by deciding how theologically incorrect those feelings are. Or we tell ourselves how much worse others have it. Basically, we shame our souls in an attempt to control what feels utterly uncontrollable.

I've spent a lot of time trying to manage my feelings. I've tried to keep them safely tucked away and brought out one at a time, only when appropriate or necessary. I was afraid of being too much for others and too much for God. I was afraid of being overwhelmed by the power of my sadness, my despair, and my fears. So I tried to hide them or ignore them. This only led to more depression.

I used to cut my arms because the physical pain was a relief compared to the pain that existed inside of me. It was a way of controlling the tirade of emotion I was so afraid to experience. I judged my feelings to be bad, wrong, and not worthy of consideration or exploration. I punished myself for feeling them in the first place. I didn't bring my pain to God because I was afraid He would punish me. Or at the very least He'd be really mad. I didn't understand that I was a much crueler judge of myself than He ever would be.

Trying to keep your emotions at bay is like trying to grasp water.

The more tightly you hold on, the more you leak. Maybe you're afraid of how your feelings will affect others. That is a realistic concern, because your feelings usually will impact those around you. However, even more than your feelings, your behavior affects the ones you love. Have you been hurtful to others in your suffering? Has your shame prevented you from being honest or vulnerable with those you love? Has your fear of being too much or not enough caused you to withdraw? All of these things are already affecting the people around you. You might not be ready to be completely open with them at the moment, because the pain is too acute. But you can bring it all to God. The more vulnerable you are with God, the more honest you can be with others. And the more honest you are, the less your feelings will have a hold on your behavior.

By encouraging you to own and confess your feelings, I am not suggesting you unleash an emotional tsunami on your family and friends. There is no need to divulge every detail of your thought process to most people. And it's not necessarily wise to do so. I'm suggesting that trying to manage your feelings rather than admitting them honestly to God impacts others anyway.

I haven't cut myself in decades. But when I experience deep suffering, I still feel ashamed of all the bad feelings that come with it. Sometimes that sadistic judge living in my head puts on her robe and strides with authority toward the bench. She grabs the gavel with ire and prepares to hand down a life sentence of self-hatred. Then I remember that I've surrendered to God. My heart is His alone to judge. So is yours. Brennan Manning wrote, "Whether positive or negative, feelings put us in touch with our true selves. They are neither good nor bad: They are simply the truth of what is going on within us. What we do with our feelings will determine whether we live lives of honesty or of deceit."[4] You don't need to decide if your feelings are good, bad, worthy of care or not. They just are. Let them be. Let Abba scoop them up in His mighty, grace-filled hands. Allow yourself and all you feel, think, and do to be held by Him.

Jesus calls you beloved. He invites you to the still waters. He offers rest. As Isaiah 42:3 beautifully shares, He will not break a bruised reed. He loves you with an everlasting love. He is not shocked or surprised by your feelings or by your desire to control them. He has a love that is so high, so wide, and so deep you cannot use it up or wear it out.

We can learn to bring our messiness to God. All at once, if we need to. If we have 27 thoughts and 45 feelings, He can take all of it. Confess. Lament. Cry out to Him. We can save our emotional tsunamis for God. One practical way we can offer these feelings to God is through journaling. To write down all the nebulous emotions that overwhelm us is to make them concrete. In a safe place, we can get all of what is happening inside of us on paper and out of our head. Because writing requires us to slow down enough to put a pen to our thoughts, it helps us to order them and articulate the jumble of emotions in words. Journal entries can become prayers of suffering and surrender and give us a way to approach God with an open, wounded heart.

Midnight is not an invitation to self-imposed cruelty. It is not designed for harsh judgment and snap decisions. While in it, Midnight will not provide a lot of perspective. It will produce more questions than answers. To try to control or judge it will only truncate the process.

I Don't Want to Wallow

Different people respond to suffering in different ways. Some people share it with others readily, others keep it to themselves. Some people cry easily. Others haven't opened a box of tissues since

1972. Some of the most joyous people I know have faced Midnights darker and deeper than I can even imagine. Their strength and courage are an inspiration. Others make Eeyore, Winnie the Pooh's gloomy companion, look like the life of the party compared to how they carry themselves in times of trouble. Who among us wouldn't want to be counted among the strong and inspiring? Who among us wants to give Eeyore a run for his money?

I've met people who have built a life around feeling sorry for themselves. They are not a fun bunch. Not the sort of folks someone who struggles with depression (or anyone, for that matter) should be hanging out with. Thankfully, they are rare (and probably don't get invited to a lot of parties). On the other hand, I have met scores of people who keep a stiff upper lip, pull themselves up by their bootstraps, and make the best of it. They refuse to wallow.

It's a tempting way to deal with suffering, by simply refusing to do so. Maybe you won't open the gift of suffering because you don't want to wallow in your circumstances. You don't want to become one of those whiny, wimpy, self-pitying downers who don't get invited to parties. After all, you have more faith than that. You know God is good. You quote Romans 8:28 with gusto. You name dozens of people who have it worse than you. You think, *I can do this!* But suffering is not the same as wallowing.

Wallowing means that a person takes all of her suffering and wraps it tightly around herself in a blanket of protection and self-pity. She tries to make everyone feel sorry for her by talking endlessly about her trials and tribulations, yet she won't allow people to speak into them, either to comfort or to challenge what they see. She claims no one understands. She blathers on and on about all that is wrong in life, but the reality is that she keeps the essence of her suffering to herself. She does not lay it down. She does not surrender. She makes it the central focus of her life. People who wallow try to control their heartbreak by mounting it on a pedestal and treating it like a priceless piece of art. Wallowers operate under the premise no one can possibly understand their suffering, not friends, not family, not therapists, and certainly not God. They create a reality that keeps them safe from the arduous work of facing their pain.

Pulling yourself up by your own bootstraps is as much an act of prideful control as wallowing in self-pity. Both are a refusal to be vulnerable to God, to allow the experience of suffering that He has, with great love, carefully allowed. With a grip of control that tight, Midnight has no room to do its mysterious and important work.

Suffering is a lonely experience. Pain can isolate. It is true that no person can understand precisely what you are going through. But the difference between wallowing and suffering is where you go with your pain. There is no need to wallow, because there is no need to suffer alone. Ever. Jesus desires to be with you in your circumstance. He understands loss, grief, suffering, and darkness because He has experienced it Himself. He was tempted (Mark 1:13), He was tired (John 4:6), and He was overwhelmed with sorrow to the point of death (Matthew 26:38). He is willing to enter into your pain if you let Him.

All Circuits Are Busy

> Save me, O God,
>   for the waters have come up to my neck.
> I sink in the miry depths,
>   where there is no foothold.
> I have come into the deep waters;
>   the floods engulf me.
> I am worn out calling for help;
>   my throat is parched.
> My eyes fail,
>   looking for my God (Psalm 69:1-3).

David speaks of his suffering as miry depths, floods, and deep waters. Forget about doing the backstroke or the freestyle. He is splashing around, dog-paddling his way to the horizon without land in sight. He is getting exhausted in trying to keep his head above water. When you are in that deep, when you are suffering that much, your whole self is involved: mentally, physically, and spiritually.

It doesn't take much for your whole body to become preoccupied with pain. You know this because you've stubbed your toe at some point in life. One tiny little toe gets hurt and every part of your body reacts. Words might flow out of your mouth that you wouldn't want your grandma to hear. In the moments after the initial stubbing, all attention is redirected to that toe. Everything is affected. You cannot think about anything else. As the pain subsides, your body and mind go back to business as usual.

Protracted physical pain keeps the mind's circuits running in one direction: toward the pain. This can lead to depression, anger, and hopelessness. It can make your world really small. When you experience injury to your body, it's difficult to think of anything else.

Emotional pain takes a serious toll too. It permeates the body as much as any physical malady, leading to a variety of illnesses. It can be debilitating. Depression, anxiety, and mental illness affect every aspect of your life. Whatever the source of suffering, you cannot disconnect your mind from your body. It's a package deal.

In Psalm 69, David describes his suffering as consuming as the ocean itself. His throat is parched. His eyes are failing. All circuits are busy. He is desperately seeking out God. The psalm says that David is searching the horizon for the One who saves, which means he can't presently see Him. It means his fear, thirst, and exhaustion are more tangible than the presence of God. Suffering clouds vision. It can carry us away. It can pull us under into life-changing darkness.

Darkness Descends

It was December 17, 1986. I was crying quietly in the backseat of my parents' car. Other than my sniffles, it was silent. We were on the freeway, driving to the Westwood Hospital Psychiatric Unit. I leaned my forehead against the cool glass of the window and looked out at the bright headlights of the northbound traffic. It seemed there were more lights on the freeway, but I wasn't sure if that was because it was the Christmas season or if I just noticed them differently because everything else was so black. The cars were moving fast, yet I felt like I was in a slow-moving nightmare, like one of those dreams in which you are running but your feet feel like lead weights and you can't seem to get anywhere.

We passed a neon cross perched on the top of a church. I can close my eyes and still see that cross, stark and bright against the night sky. It mocked me, looking grotesquely happy in all its neon splendor. I was sure that whatever special club that cross represented didn't include me. I was outside of anything that belonged. My breath fogged the glass, and I closed my eyes.

I was a senior in high school and had been in counseling since September. I was taking antidepressant medication that (kind of) managed my overwhelming feelings of depression and sadness. The medication offered in 1986 was effective in preventing me from committing suicide, but it made my thoughts slow and my behavior slightly robotic. It also made me gain about 20 pounds. Clearly, my chances of being voted homecoming queen were low. High school is not necessarily the best time to be a depressed, robotic redhead. (Come to think of it, is there ever a time for that socially pernicious combo? Probably not.)

A few hours before, I was at the psychiatrist's office for my monthly check-in. I could not stop crying. I refused to answer any of his questions. I didn't want to be with him or anyone for that matter, yet I was terrified to be alone. He asked me to promise I would not hurt myself. I would not look at him or respond. He asked me again. Silence. He got up, ushered my mom into the room, and told her he wanted to admit me to a psychiatric hospital right away. He told her to take me home, help me pack, and meet him at the hospital in two hours. I just sat there and cried. I still didn't say a word.

I remember the admittance process was arduous and humiliating. The admitting nurse (who I'm pretty sure was in a motorcycle gang) asked a profuse number of invasive questions about my drinking, smoking, drug use, and physical condition—in front of my mother, no less. I gave one-word answers as often as possible. After what felt like the Spanish Inquisition, the nurse took me to another room, where I was stripped naked and searched for contraband. For some reason, the nurse kept yelling at me. I'm not sure what I did to deserve her ire since I was nearly catatonic, but a warm fuzzy she was not. After I got dressed, I was given about 30 seconds to say good-bye to my folks before being locked in a small room with soft walls, a cot, and a very tiny window.

I was finally alone.

Away from the concerned face of my psychiatrist.

Away from the shame of the strip search.

Away from my frightened and confused parents.

Away from Nurse Sharon's brusque, accusatory interrogation.

Alone.

I looked out that small window at the night sky. There was a full moon gazing back at me, glowing as brightly as the neon cross. I remember staring at it and wondering if God knew where I was or if He cared. In my half-formed thoughts, I *felt* the question more than asked it. Are You there, God? Do You see me? After running my hands along the padded walls and considering the Midnight sky a bit longer, I decided He knew exactly where I was. And He didn't care.

The Invitation

This is the part of the story where I should describe how God showed up in that terribly dark period of my life. This is the moment where I should share all the lessons I learned and how grateful I am for that experience. Except I won't. Not yet, anyway. Not because God didn't eventually make Himself known. He did. And not because I didn't learn a lot. I did. But if I jump to all the important lessons and blessings I can look back on and see with clarity on the other side of my pain, I am diminishing the power of Midnight. If the only gifts we discover are the ones on the other side of suffering, it makes the whole concept of Midnight irrelevant. We need to explore the unwrapped, undone, unfinished places of this faith journey and discover the grace waiting for us in the center of our suffering. This is not a book about how to get *through* the darkest parts of life; it's about how to be *in* them.

The utter aloneness I experienced that night and in that time of my life makes my heart ache even now. Maybe it's not an actual ache. Maybe it's more the memory of an ache. Either way, just because I can look back on it and tell you about it doesn't mean it's wrapped up in a neat little package for me now. It definitely wasn't wrapped up for me then.

Midnight is about getting comfortable with the feelings we don't want to feel and the questions about God we don't want to ask. It is stopping down in our pain long enough to consider that Midnight is not just counting down the minutes until the sun rises; it is an invitation to find God in the darkness. Suffering, as awful as it is, is often our entryway into a deeper relationship with Jesus Christ. If we spend our whole time looking for a way out of it, we miss the radiance within it.

Suffering clears away distractions and whittles the world down to the immediate.

Walls. A cot. A room. Suffering forces us to be intensely present, aware of almost nothing else but our immediate circumstances. Pain strip-searches our insides and removes the shallow comforts we cling to in ordinary circumstances. We are left bare.

God knows you just want the suffering to stop. But you have been invited to more than a life of circumventing pain. When you've stopped trying to make sense of it, when you cease to judge it or avoid it, you have nothing, "no thing" left. And no thing in the hands of God is the beginning of "some thing." Midnight is an invitation to offer your no thing—your nothing—to God, because it's all you have. Nothing in your hands becomes despair. But your nothing in the hands of God is the beginning of intimacy.

The Gift of Suffering

> It is natural for us to wish that God had designed for us
> a less glorious and less arduous destiny; but then we are
> wishing not for love, but for less.
> —C.S. Lewis[5]

I want so much to look the part of a humble, serene, suffering saint. I want so much to have a look of contentment on my face and tranquility in my heart. I want to declare to the Lord with certainty and conviction, "Not what I will, but what You will." I want to look faithful. Even more, I want to *be* faithful. In the face of pain, I want to behave like I actually trust God. But when I look in the mirror and take in my reflection, I see puffy eyes from crying, a mouth pulled down, and lines upon my forehead, drawn by worry and fear. I see a very small child, vulnerable and naked with desperation. I don't like what I see, and I don't like what I feel.

Romans 8:16-18 tells us that the children of God will share in Christ's sufferings. My shoulders slump and I am quite defeated when I imagine I need to suffer like Christ did. I can barely put on my mascara when things are tough. How can I possibly be like Him?

But we are not called to do *what* Christ did; we are called to suffer *as* He did. Christ's sufferings stand alone. You are not called to replicate what cannot be replicated. And the work Jesus did on the cross—taking on the sin of the world that we might be reconciled to God—cannot be replicated by mere mortals anyway, which is why He alone could do it in the first place. The suffering of Christ doesn't need to be replicated. It was done once, for all.

Suffering as Christ did means trusting wholly and with naked vulnerability in the Father's plan. It means you set aside the temptation to wallow, to fight, to battle on your own, or to try and take control of something you have no right to control. It would be useless in your hands anyway. God is not demanding stoicism or pensive resignation. He doesn't care if your mascara smears. True surrender will invite suffering because you are no longer under the illusion that you are in control. God is asking you to trust Him with this Midnight.

The fullness of trusting God is laying bare your pain to Him without a filter of shame and judgment about how you should be feeling. It is not preemptively packaging your pain in more acceptable wrapping. Trusting God involves a confession of complete abandon. Jesus Christ, in the face of suffering, was not stoic. He was not resigned. Sweat, in the form of great drops of blood falling to the ground, poured from His forehead. He was in agony. Jesus was, in the words of Scripture, "sorrowful and troubled" and "overwhelmed with sorrow to the point of death" (Matthew 26:37-38).

In His pain, His vulnerability, and His complete trust in His Father, He laid bare His requests, specifically, "If it is possible, may this cup be taken from me" (verse 39). This is the suffering of Christ. This is the Midnight you are invited to.

Sharing in Christ's sufferings means you give over complete control to an uncontrollable God. You declare "not as I will, but as You will" with puffy eyes and an aching heart. There is no false resignation in your words. It is a shaky but sincere offering of trust. Suffering as Christ means you remain vulnerable to His plans and willing to stay put when everything in you wants to run.

It is Daniel sitting among the lions.

It is Joseph lying at the bottom of a well.

It is David hiding in a cave.

It is Mary standing at the foot of the cross and watching her son die in agony.

It is Paul writing from inside prison walls.

If Midnight is an invitation to intimacy with God, suffering is the envelope. There is something specific that happens in this process that will not happen any other way. The gift of suffering is an intimate communion with God. It is taking a journey that will be dark and troubling at times. But this path has been well worn by others who have taken it before you. They have experienced Midnight and have found Christ there with them in it. This is your invitation to find Him there too.

There is not a place in Midnight that Jesus has not traveled. There is not one corner of this place unexamined by Him. He goes before you, He is with you, and He's got your back. Isaiah 53:3 describes the Messiah as "a man of suffering, and familiar with pain." He knows the terrain of Midnight because He has traveled it Himself.

Sometimes Jesus is hard to see in the throes of Midnight. But He is there. The gift of suffering is that you can reach out in this darkness and find His hand reaching out for yours every time. You may be feeling lost, but He is not. Midnight is as familiar to Him as daylight. He can see you clearly. He knows the purpose of this time. He is not asking for a great mountain of faith, just a tiny mustard seed and a willingness to offer Him your deepest pain. He is asking for your hand, emptied of anything else, so He can grasp it and walk with you in and through this.

The gift of suffering is discovering that He is not horrified by the feelings that horrify you. You have a safe place to go with your anguish. You don't need to control it or carry it alone, because in His hands, the deepest, most fearful parts of yourself will not overwhelm or destroy you. You are here in this sacred darkness, trusting Him with all that breaks your heart. There is no thing between you and God. You are part of the radiant Midnight, and this is a time ordained by Him. God is working, and it is good even when it feels terrible. Let's journey on together.

MOONLIGHT MEDITATIONS

- How have you coped with your feelings in this Midnight?

- Have you tried to control your feelings, clean them up, or judge them instead of bringing them to God?

- How have the people in your life been affected by your Midnight?

- How might this time of suffering be the beginning of something new?

EVENING STROLL

- Write a letter to God. Tell Him everything, and I mean everything. How you feel about your circumstances. How you feel about Him. What you fear most. Consider how your pain has affected you physically and spiritually. Be as honest as possible. When you are done, offer all of what you wrote to the Lord. Make your letter a gift to Him. Give Him your words, your emotions, and your honesty. In the process, you are offering Him yourself.

4

LONG STARRY NIGHTS

Are we there yet?

EVERY KID ON ANY VACATION EVER

Vincent van Gogh is one of the world's most famous painters. His canvases are thick and craggy with layers of paint that bring his works alive with color and movement. He sketched and painted peasants, fields, irises, sunflowers, and even shoes. He found extraordinary beauty in ordinary places. He made inanimate objects sing with life. Sometimes the music of his work was catchy and upbeat, at other times they were heart-wrenching ballads of anguish. When he died in 1890, he left behind more than 900 paintings and scores of letters to a variety of people, including his beloved brother and benefactor, Theo van Gogh. In one of his letters to Theo, Vincent wrote, "I long so much to make beautiful things. But beautiful things require effort—and disappointment and perseverance."[1]

Has this time in Midnight left you wondering if all the disappointment and perseverance will lead to anything beautiful? Does it feel like time is ticking and nothing has changed, moved forward, or healed? Does your heart long to know that something beautiful is being made from what looks like ashes? Have you been asking God "Are we there yet?"

A Little While

Time is a remarkable thing. A weekend in New York—time sprints. A dentist appointment—time slows to a shuffle. Bring on the darkness of struggle, heartbreak, or grief—time puts up its feet and takes a nap. We can tell time, but we cannot tell time what to do. It won't be bossed around by the likes of us.

Have you heard about Chinese water torture? A person is strapped down and water is dripped onto his forehead a drop at a time until, on the brink of madness, the poor sap spills his guts. When you are in the throes of Midnight, time feels cruel. It is a slow, steady drip of anguish. It drops one minute at a time into a chasm of pain that threatens to pull you under. If it were possible to drown one drop at a time, Midnight could make it happen. It is the Chinese water torture of the heart.

The apostle Peter wrote, "After you have suffered *a little while*, the God of all grace, who has called you to his eternal glory in Christ, will himself restore, confirm, strengthen, and establish you" (1 Peter 5:10 ESV, emphasis added). This verse makes clear that suffering will eventually end. That is great news, but it's fuzzy in its time frame, which is highly unsettling. After all, this verse is inspired by God, the Alpha and Omega who has no beginning and no end, the great I Am who is not limited by time or place and is by His very nature eternal. So if you're a bit circumspect about what "a little while" might be, I am too. Sometimes it doesn't seem like God's watch and ours are synchronized.

How Long?

> How long, LORD? Will you forget me forever?
>   How long will you hide your face from me?
> How long must I wrestle with my thoughts
>   and day after day have sorrow in my heart?

How long will my enemy triumph over me? (Psalm 13:1-2).

David begins Psalm 13 with some poignant questions for God. He has been waiting so long for God, he wonders out loud if his Abba has forgotten him altogether. At the very least, he's sure God is playing a frustrating game of hide-and-seek. He has been crying out for some time, and the Lord seems to be busy with other stuff. David is losing morale. He's looked at the last days, weeks, and months on his calendar and doesn't like what he sees. David has been in the same place, surrounded by the same problems, and feeling the same way for far too long. It's wearing on him physically, mentally, and emotionally.

Moreover, he's not only marking time by his own sense of loneliness and frustration, he's delineating it by observing what's going on around him. That's even more of a bummer. His enemies are flourishing while he is feeling like a chump. His enemies are experiencing the sweet taste of victory while David wrestles, sorrows, and loses. People are moving on. Moving ahead. Moving forward. They have energy to go to the gym, and they are in the best small groups at church. They laugh and have fun. Their cars don't smell like feet and french fries. Their Instagram photos are artistic and interesting. Meanwhile, David has been stuck in the same place for much longer than is fair, watching his enemies flourish, and he's beginning to wonder if God even remembers he's there.

Are you wondering the same thing? Has it felt like you've been in this Midnight for far too long, watching far too many people soaking up the daylight, taking great selfies? Do you even remember what it was like before the darkness of your present circumstances? Are you wondering how much longer this Midnight will last?

Suffering sucks the life out of you. It tears down instead of builds up. It is winter, not spring. It is uprooting, not planting. It is mourn-ing, not dancing. If your circumstances have been the same for some time, and your heart cries out "How long, Lord?" and you cannot see the end in sight, then time itself appears to be a punishment. It feels cruel and unkind, like sandpaper rubbing away your hope.

But as we've established, Midnight isn't the place where you'll have a lot of perspective. Your vision is clouded, and even if there were an exit right in front of you, you might not see it in all the sur-rounding darkness. If you do not trust this Midnight and the time ordained for you to stay here, your mind will play tricks on you and you will begin to believe that the Lord has indeed forgotten you. And time will become your enemy.

The Guy Who Lives in the Basement

For me, depression is like a lumbering, mean-spirited cousin who came to visit for an afternoon and ended up moving into my basement. I will sit down for a warm cup of coffee first thing in the morning, and before I'm even fully awake, depression comes galumphing up the stairs and plops down at the table, disturbing the peaceful pace of the moment with his heavy presence. Depres-sion sucks the air out of the room and makes it hard to breathe. He has a stench. When he begins to speak, he talks slowly and delib-erately. He tells me things with such confidence that I listen with-out questioning the veracity of his words. I sip my coffee, and his hot, stinking breath creates beads of sweat on my nose because he is leaning so close to my face. I am frozen with fear, with intimida-tion, with the heaviness of every word depression utters. He creeps into the places of my mind and heart that are supposed to be private and personal. He violates them. He doesn't care about me. I think he likes to humiliate me with his words. He is cruel. And because he's a cousin—not a stranger—he is familiar with my history, family dynamics, and long-ago-set patterns imprinted in my heart. He uses his knowledge to entangle truth and deception. He confuses me.

He wants to take my faith, the people I love, and all that is good in my life and make me believe they were never mine in the first place. He roams freely in my home. He eats the food in the refrigerator. He drops crumbs on the clean floors. He leaves the toilet seat up. He's a nightmare house guest, and I cannot seem to get him to move out.

There are seasons when he hibernates. He stays down in the basement, and while I might hear him shuffling around or bumping into the walls once in a while, he doesn't make an actual appearance. If he's been absent for quite a while, I let myself believe that maybe he slipped out the basement window and moved on to another place. Then one day I pour my cup of coffee, like every other morning, and I turn around and find him seated at my kitchen table once again, smug and arrogant, ready to rock and roll.

The benefit of having lived with depression for most of my life is that I've had time to become familiar with his habits and tricks. He's a shifty type, but he relies on a few standard taunts, using them over and over. He lacks originality. I'm finally seeing his pattern. I still can't get him to move out, but I'm not letting him have the run of the house any more.

Depression uses two basic strategies to keep me entangled in his lies. He will convince me it's always been this bad, hard, dark, terrible, etc. or that it will always be this bad, hard, dark, terrible, etc. He speaks with such authority, it's hard to completely disregard his words. But I'm learning.

Midnight is when all that haunts us emerges from the basement. It may not be depression that barges its way into our life, but he's got a lot of cousins, and I bet it will be one of them: anger, fear, discontentedness, self-worthlessness. All those guys hang out together.

It will be hard to remember what daylight was like. What it was to feel warmth on our skin and see blue skies above. It will feel like it's always been this way. We might begin to feel hopeless. Because when we believe the guy in the basement more than we believe God's faithfulness, our heart will be affected.

Hard Times, Harder Hearts

The book of Exodus tells the story of Moses and the Israelites. In the beginning of this book, the Israelites, God's chosen people, have been slaves in Egypt for generations. They cried out to their God and asked for freedom, and after about four hundred years, the Lord decided He'd had enough of Egyptian shenanigans. He elected Moses to lead the Israelites to freedom. After plagues and pestilence of epic proportions, the Egyptian pharaoh finally released the Israelites to Moses. From there, events took place that still show up in Hollywood movies. Seas parted. Women sang songs. Moses held his staff and led the people out of Egypt. The bad guys lost. It was awesome.

From there the story gets a little sticky. Once all the drama settled down, the Israelites found themselves taking the long route to the Promised Land. They were free from slavery but wandering in the middle of the desert. I say wandering because that's how it's usually described by preachers and commentators and even Scripture. I'm sure that is how it felt to the Israelites. But that's not exactly the entire truth of the matter. Not in the beginning, at least. They did indeed walk through the desert. However, every step was led by God. Each place they went, every grain of sand they tread upon, every place they spent the night was ordained. It was all part of God's plan for them (Deuteronomy 2:7).

In the beginning, with the memory of walking through the Red Sea fresh in their minds, the desert wasn't too bad. But after a while all that sand started to get to them. They started to complain.

Incessantly. Then, while Moses was in a business meeting with God on Mount Sinai, the Israelites completely lost their minds. They built a golden calf and started to worship it. They decided the golden calf was more predictable than God. They had to choose between faith and sight and they chose sight. They decided the time was up for Midnight and tried to force daylight to return through their own strength. So they built something they could see and touch. It made them feel strong and in control. That was when their wandering really began.

God loved His people with an everlasting love. He cared about their sunburns and cold desert nights, so He provided a cloud by day to shield them and a fire by night to warm them. He fed them manna and brought them leaders to guide them. But the Israelites were not satisfied with those things. Even though God provided for them every single day in that awful desert place, they were still vastly unhappy and distrustful of God's plan because it wasn't what they expected.

When the Israelites complained about the trek and, worse yet, decided to draw their strength from a giant metal statue, God didn't smite them or send down lightning bolts, although He considered it (Exodus 32:9-10). Instead, He decided to teach them what they needed to understand by giving them the gift of time. Forty long years. I don't think the Israelites saw those years as a gift. True, the 40-year detour was a consequence for their awful behavior. They were not going to enter the Promised Land because of their distrust and disobedience (Numbers 14:21-22). Regardless, those 40 years were from God, which means that even in the midst of it feeling really bad, it offered good things.

Now, if I were wandering around in the desert for a long time, I might get a bit cranky too. Scratch that. I promise you I would get cranky. I am a redhead. My skin burns easily, and I feel faint if

I spend too much time in the sun. Also, I sweat profusely. It would be altogether unattractive and inconvenient to be tromping through vast regions of nothingness.

When your feet ache and your clothes stick to your back and you feel faint from exhaustion, how do you avoid becoming the next generation of complaining, whining, obnoxious Israelites? How do you trust this time of Midnight, when nothing is clear and everything radiates with uncompromising heat? Do you just suck it up and keep trekking, convinced that you must keep your hurt (and, in the process, your heart) locked up and stuffed away for fear of retribution from a God who invited you into this Midnight in the first place? No. May it never be.

God didn't punish the Israelites with 40 years of desert wanderings because they complained about the heat. Crankiness, while unattractive, is a human condition that comes with sunburn, blisters, and exhaustion. When we are grouchy, it means we need to soak our feet, take some Advil, and get some sleep. God is not preoccupied with our crankiness, although it is an indicator that something more pressing might be going on. His main concern is for our heart. The Lord wants it soft and pliable and workable. Through His prophet Ezekiel, the Lord promised His people what they needed most: "I will give you a new heart and put a new spirit in you; I will remove from you your heart of stone and give you heart of flesh" (36:26). God wants a soft heart, one that is pliable and teachable and inclined toward Him. He has good and loving plans for us, and He has fashioned us for good work. He is faithful to produce these things, but He won't do it quickly. We are too precious to rush this. It might feel like wandering. But we are not. Every step, every pain, every place we travel in this Midnight is ordained by Him.

Keeping a soft heart in this time will allow you to hear His voice in the darkness. He will whisper words of encouragement and kindness and redemption into your ears as He refines your soul and sews up the places that have been ripped and torn. He is the great surgeon, and He is doing careful work. He will take the time to do it well, to do it right. He has given you the gift of time because it is where He moves to heal your deepest wounds. This time is sacred. A soft heart, held safely in His capable hands, will keep you still while He does the necessary surgery.

The downside to having a soft heart is that it can be hurt. Unlike a stony heart, it will feel pain. You will cry out when its tender parts are touched. You will bleed and bruise. Your soft heart will not feel strong. It will feel like it is going to hurt forever. You might even long for a stony heart, one that doesn't damage so easily. But stony hearts cannot experience the love of God the way a soft heart can. Sure, they might be tougher, but they cannot feel God's touch.

Time can either harden or soften you. You can be strong and hard or vulnerable and soft. The soft heart feels pain that leads to growth, while the hard heart feels bitterness that makes it shrink and detract from the fullness of God.

God wanted the Israelites to stay out of the Promised Land because they allowed their hearts to harden right along with the callouses on their feet. They believed their time in the desert was for nothing, that it was not valuable. They treated time like an enemy instead of trusting in its powerful ability to produce contented faith. They grew apathetic and angry toward the God who loved them more than anything else in all creation. If the Israelites entered the Promised Land with stony hearts, then the entire point of them being there would have been missed. They would have grapes and figs and milk and honey, but they wouldn't have hearts soft enough to hear from the Lover of their souls. They would have everything they wanted but nothing they truly needed (Exodus 33:1-13).

For 40 years God let time do what it was created to do: bring softening, reconciliation, and hope. The time in the desert didn't just pass by; it created something new. The years in the desert changed a pattern of thinking established by four hundred years of slavery. He waited until the generation of Israelites who escaped Egypt had died (with the exception of Joshua and Caleb), and He allowed their children to enter instead. The children were different from their parents; they had a story of freedom instead of chains. They didn't know anything else but sand and sun. It may not have been paradise, but they had nothing to compare it to. Most important, their hearts were not hardened against God.

Turning away from God when you are in pain is like eating french fries to deal with your cholesterol problem. The short-term result is deep-fried deliciousness with a side of ranch dressing. Those fries might make you feel better. You relax. You feel satisfied. Aren't relaxation and satisfaction good for the heart? Yep. But the long-term effect of those fries? Not so much.

Midnight can be vast. We cannot see the end of it when we are in the middle. It will leave us feeling weak and exhausted. We'll be tempted to draw the wrong conclusions about our pain and the time we are spending in it. We will wonder if God has left us to languish in pain. We'll imagine He's forgotten us. We might want to forget God in the process too. Maybe we will decide to traverse this Midnight on our own, because depending upon a God who will not remove us from this place is a lot more painful than using our own strength to pry ourselves out. We need to guard our heart at Midnight.

That cousin who lives in the basement will tell you in no uncertain terms that God has abandoned you. He will tell you that God hates you and that God is cruel and/or mean. He will tell you that God is not to be trusted. He will use your pain as proof that what he says is true. He will tell you it's going to be like this forever. He will insist it has always been like this. He will take your sacred, God-given, holy time—your Midnight—and he will try to make it something it is not. He will plant the seeds of bitterness in your heart and water them daily with doubts, entitlements, and temptations.

But he doesn't get to do that if you don't allow it. You might be in pain, confused, and lost in this desert Midnight far longer than you ever thought possible. But you are not without resources. God provides a cloud of shade to protect you from the searing heat. He's given you fire to protect and warm you when it gets cold. He has provided manna to nourish you. He has provided for you by giving you what your heart needs most: He has given you His whole self, all of Him. He is with you in this time, therefore, you can trust it is not senseless. Every step you take in this place is planned and accounted for, and God will use this time to draw you to Himself. Moreover, you don't have to keep your pain to yourself. He'll make room for your doubts, complaints, and imaginations of impending doom, especially when you cry out from a sincere, soft heart.

A Corrosive or a Balm

> Look on me and answer, LORD my God.
> Give light to my eyes, or I will sleep in death,
> and my enemy will say "I have overcome him,"
> and my foes will rejoice when I fall (Psalm 13:3-4).

After starting Psalm 13 with several pointed questions for the Lord, David flat out starts to beg. I like that David is slightly histrionic in these verses. He plots out the worst-case scenario and presents that to God. Death is imminent. His enemies will win. He will fall. His enemies will rejoice. This is highly encouraging to me because, like David, I am the master of the worst-case scenario. I've planned my funeral hundreds of times. I've imagined what will be said, who will attend, and what I will be wearing. I just know my children will wander aimlessly through life because I am not there to dispense profound wisdom. I'm confident my house will be foreclosed on because my husband never memorized the passwords to our online bank account. And surely no one will remember to feed the dog.

Scripture shows us that David is not a caricature of a person, pious and faithful and at peace in his heart no matter what the circumstances. He was a real man. He lived on this earth and felt the sun on his face and felt the cold at night. He was anguished and he hurt and he doubted and he complained. He was a worst-case-scenario kind of guy too. But David knew what to do with all of that hysteria. He didn't have a lot of answers, but he knew where to go with his questions, and it kept his heart soft.

Time can serve as a corrosive or a balm. It can erode or it can heal. If you take your pain and your questions and your fear and tuck them safely away, you are not allowing God to work in this sacred time. It's tantamount to sticking your broken-down car in the garage and hoping that time will fix it. Your car, like your heart, won't fix itself; it needs to be worked on by someone who knows what is broken. Time only works for you when it is in the hands of the One who knows what to do with it. Hardening your heart might make you feel stronger, but it will not lead you to the place God intends for you to go. When you turn to Him with your deepest worries and heartaches in your Midnight, you are taking steps to ensure your heart will not grow hard with bitterness. You are trusting that this time is important and intended and will lead to morning. Even when you can't remember what morning feels like.

Remembrance

I have a terrible memory. Seriously. If I had a nickel for every time I walked into a room without remembering why, I'd be writing to you from my private island just next to Johnny Depp's island. Unfortunately, no one is paying me nickels to wander around the house, mumbling to myself and retracing my steps. I forget to return messages. I forget appointments. I forget the meal I put on the stove to cook 30 minutes earlier. I am jarred back to reality when the smoke alarm goes off.

Of course, there are certain things I do remember. Like that time a kid put duct tape in my hair in the seventh grade. Or that time I did a cartwheel in elementary school and forgot to wear bike shorts beneath my plaid skirt. I know *The Flintstones* theme song by heart. Yep. I remember those little gems like yesterday. But the laundry I threw into the washing machine a half hour ago? I won't remember it until I smell something weird and musty two days from now. I cannot even remember stuff that I really, really want to remember, like when my kids were little or my first few years of marriage. It's all a blur.

Memory is a curious thing. Why do we remember some events and not others? Why is it that some of the most pivotal times in our lives are hazy flashbacks that never quite come into focus and yet random anecdotal incidents are burned into us forever? I have no idea. But memory serves an important purpose. It reflects the significance of time.

My husband, Danny, and I visited the 9-11 Memorial in New York a while back. It was a haunting, life-affirming, moving experience. In the midst of the outside grounds, there is a Callery pear tree surrounded by a small three-foot fence. The tree originally grew near the Twin Towers long before the horrifying terrorist attacks in 2001. It was found in the rubble afterward, badly burned. Its damage reflected what the whole country was experiencing. It was nursed back to health by the New York Department of Parks and Recreation and is now back home, planted once again in the outside perimeter of where the Twin Towers once stood. The tree is called the Survivor Tree. The 9-11 Memorial and Museum website provides this information: "New, smooth limbs [are] extended from the gnarled stumps, creating a visible demarcation between the tree's past and present. Today, the tree stands as a living reminder of resilience, survival and rebirth."[2] The Survivor Tree reflects how time has the remarkable ability to bring new life to what has been crushed. It is a testament to the importance of memory. The new growth mingled with the scarred trunk represents all that was lost and all that persisted. It is a declaration of resilience and renewal.

When all is said and done, you may not want to remember this Midnight. You might be looking forward to the day when your face will be warmed by the sun and you'll clearly see where you are and where you are going. You might be confident you will never look back on this time with fondness or affection. You know you will not yearn for this time again, and you will not want to recall it with any vivid detail. Midnight is hard, so it makes sense if you don't want to remember it.

But at the risk of exasperating or alarming you, I have to tell you that this will probably not be the only Midnight you experience in your life. The truth is that Midnight comes around with some regularity, which is why it's so important to remember each one. You will most likely pass this way again, so you might as well slow down enough to notice your surroundings. Suffering needs to become familiar terrain.

As disorienting and disappointing as it can be, this season is vitally important to your soul. God is carefully repairing, replacing, and renewing your story into something glorious and radiant. Like a child being knit in the darkness of the womb, you are being fashioned into someone who will burst forth with new life. It's hard to imagine when you are hurting so deeply, but you can trust this awful, painful, breathtaking time. God is not letting it pass untouched by His healing hands. He is growing new branches. Allow this journey to have a permanent place in your heart. Honor its significance. Remember these days that drag on far too long and the nights when you cannot sleep. Do not ignore the depth of what God is doing by locking it away once it's over.

When Midnight becomes familiar territory, it loses some of its terror. And when we are not so scared, we can begin to discover the beauty of this sacred season. Our hearts are created to seek out beauty because our hearts are created to seek out God. Where beauty exists, God is present.

Once daylight comes, your memory will begin to fade. You might reflect on this time with memories that are twisted and inaccurate. It might become all bad or not as bad as it really was. Either way, you could forget the significance of this crucible. You will need these memories, because Midnight is as cyclical as the moon itself.

The Israelite experience of slavery in Egypt was horrendous. But even when the Israelites were free, their hearts remained captive. They grumbled and fussed and whined in the desert. They remembered their slavery in a twisted and inaccurate way. They reimagined it to reinforce the story they told themselves: God had abandoned them, and Moses didn't know what he was doing. In Exodus 16:3 they said, "If only we had died by the LORD's hand in Egypt! There we sat around pots of meat and ate all the food we wanted, but you have brought us out into this desert to starve this entire assembly of death." Now, I know the wilderness wandering was no picnic, but for heaven's sake they had been *slaves* for four hundred years. They worked seven days a week and had no freedom of their own. Sure, they were fed, but only so they could keep working. And yet somehow the Israelites are harkening back to the "good ol' days" that never happened. Why did they recount a distorted version of their slavery more readily than they remembered walking through the Red Sea? Why didn't they recall God's faithfulness when it hung in a cloud of fire right over their heads? They might as well have been back in chains. Their bodies were free, but their minds were not. They did not carry the power of what they had witnessed with them, and it corroded their relationship with God.

As a result, some 40 years later, when it was time for the children of the Israelites to finally enter the Promised Land, God did something both familiar and new. Just as He parted the waters of the Red Sea for their parents, God parted the Jordan River in order to let the next generation of Israelites into the Promised Land. Only this time, He had them take some souvenirs.

> When the whole nation had finished crossing the Jordan, the LORD said to Joshua, "Choose twelve men from among the people, one from each tribe, and tell them to take up twelve stones from the middle of the Jordan, from right where the priests are standing, and carry them over with you and put them down at the place where you stay tonight."
>
> So Joshua called together the twelve men he had appointed from the Israelites, one from each tribe, and said to them, "Go over before the ark of the LORD your God into the middle of the Jordan. Each of you is to take up a stone on his shoulder, according to the number of the tribes of the Israelites, to serve as a sign among you. In the future, when your children ask you, 'What do these stones mean?' tell them that the flow of the Jordan was cut off before the ark of the covenant of the LORD. When it crossed the Jordan, the waters of the Jordan were cut off. These stones are to be a memorial to the people of Israel forever" (Joshua 4:1-7).

God wanted the children of Israel to remember His faithfulness because He knew there were more Midnights ahead. He wanted them to have stones of remembrance, taken from the very center of their crossing so they could never again deny His presence in their time of need. They had physical proof that told them otherwise.

> But I trust in your unfailing love;
>   my heart rejoices in your salvation.
> I will sing the LORD's praise,
>   for he has been good to me (Psalm 13:5-6).

David closes Psalm 13 with a memory of God's goodness. His circumstances have not changed since he cried out "How long, LORD?" but that doesn't prevent him from recalling the Lord's goodness. David trusts that God, in His unfailing love, is doing something precious and important in time. He has stones of remembrance—past experiences with God that prove His faithfulness. When he cannot recall what sunlight felt like on his face, he can still remember God's goodness.

Evidence of Midnight

"Time heals all wounds" is a lovely thought, and like most annoying sayings is somewhat true. Over time a minor scrape will heal with no evidence it ever existed. But a deep wound? Time can make the wound smaller, easier to manage, and eventually seal it over, but it will always leave evidence the wound was made. We are forever different from the damage this life brings. Can we find healing? Yes. Are we the same as before? No. Scars have been formed that will always remain. The bigger the wound, the deeper the scar.

After Jesus endured the torture, humiliation, and agony of crucifixion and after He was dead for three days, He came back. He wasn't a ghost. He wasn't an apparition. He was there in the flesh for all to see. His understandably freaked-out disciples had *no* idea what to make of it. "Am I seeing this right?" they wondered. "Is this *the* Jesus? *Our* Jesus?" In response, Jesus showed them His scars.

Jesus Christ bears the scars that came with His sacrifice on the cross. Our omnipresent, all-knowing Creator, the great I Am, has been affected by His time with us. He felt heat and cold, hunger and loneliness. He spent time working, playing, fishing, walking. After His horrific death, He had the power to remove those scars and erase any evidence of His naked humiliation, torture, and death on the cross. And yet they remain.

God, who lives outside of time—the Alpha and Omega—has allowed Himself to be altered by what He experienced in time, in the era He spent walking the dust and dirt of Israel. He has deemed those scars worthy to keep. They are the scars of Midnight.

The deeper the wounds of this time, the more pronounced your scars will be. But Jesus demonstrates that scars are important. They are the remembrance stones for your soul. Let them remind you that you were here in this place and let them point to the healing that is taking place.

The Gift of Time

> Time is not a luxury, but a necessity.
> —Henry Cloud[3]

This darkened place of Midnight is a space where God is present and purposeful. He is keenly aware of your pain. He has walked in your shoes and felt the soul-crushing depths of it. He will not allow one moment more in this place than necessary. But this time is, indeed, necessary.

Time marks both growth and demise. In the hands of God, the

gift of time creates mountains and rivers and the Grand Canyon. It forges new paths and opens new roads and rebuilds what has been ruined and discovers what has been lost. It is God's most patient, careful gift. He will not rush through this, because you are far too precious to Him and this work is far too complex. The gift of time is that, in God's hands, every second counts. No breath, moment, or tear is wasted or left undiscovered. Time is His greatest tool for healing and wholeness.

At your lowest, the enemy of your soul will try to convince you it's been this horrible forever and will be this horrible forever. He will try to harden your heart through bitterness and impatience. He's a liar. Keep a soft heart through the muck and mire of worry and frustration so you can hear the words of comfort and grace God is speaking while He does His work.

The passing of time is proof that Midnight doesn't last forever. There were new dawns and lazy afternoons and breathtaking sunsets before all of this. There will be again. Sometimes those beautiful skies are hard to remember when you can't see much of anything. But it doesn't make those bright places less true. Your Midnight will end. Daylight will emerge. You may have deep scars added to your heart, but they are remembrance stones of your survival and God's faithfulness. And when another Midnight does arrive sometime down the road, it will never be exactly like the one now. Remember this time because it will never come this way again.

Although Vincent van Gogh created some of the most iconic, revered, and memorable paintings in all of history, he sold only one painting during his lifetime. One.[4] Though he persisted in his endeavors and worked tirelessly at his craft, the time van Gogh dedicated to his passion didn't produce a lot of outward reward. And yet his effort, perseverance, and dedication have been honored by the passage of time. Presently, his paintings are worth millions, if not considered priceless altogether. The years have opened people's eyes to the beauty that was always there.

About a year before he died, van Gogh was living in a sanitarium, wracked with depression and anxiety. He often was not well enough to even walk outside in the asylum gardens. His room was small and had only one barred window. At night he'd look at the stars, waiting for the pain to pass.[5] I imagine he felt like it was taking forever.

Van Gogh didn't paint during those long nights; it was too dark. He had to wait for the daylight to come. He needed enough light to see the canvas. But he knew there was beauty in the darkness. He held the memory of Midnight in his heart and kept the view from his window as a stone of remembrance. Inspired by what he experienced in the darkness, Van Gogh created his most famous work: *Starry Night*.[6] Painting it most likely required perseverance, effort, and disappointment. But it was from his time in Midnight that he created something exquisitely beautiful. God is doing the same in you.

MOONLIGHT MEDITATIONS

- What is present in your life that has been there far too long?
- What wounds have been made that could leave permanent scars?
- Is your heart still soft toward God in this time or has it hardened?
- How has the condition of your heart affected your Midnight?

EVENING STROLL

- Find a stone of remembrance that represents this Midnight. It might be an actual stone or it could be a candle, photograph, or something unique to your current situation. Any kind of physical proof that you've been in this Midnight will work. Next, write down what is happening presently, even the hard parts, because you will not be able to recall this time with clarity later on. Put the note and remembrance in a place where you will see them often. Allow them to represent this sacred, heartbreaking, important time when God is doing mighty things. After this time has passed (and it will), you will have proof that it happened and, even better, that you survived it.

5

THE SILENT GOD

My nerves are bad tonight. Yes, bad. Stay with me.
Speak to me. Why do you never speak? Speak.

T.S. ELIOT[1]

Maturity and my mother have taught me to have a bit more wisdom than to simply go with the first feeling that comes to me. I understand that feelings are not facts. I don't allow my feelings to rule the day. I know how to suck it up. But if I were to strip away all the maturity that being a grown-up requires, I would react to most things the same as a four-year-old child. Christmas morning? Pure joy and excitement. Clean up a mess? Let the whining begin. Floss my teeth? That's boring! Play date with a friend? Jumping up and down! Wait for something? Collapse to the floor and throw a tantrum.

Most of us don't like to wait. Whether it's a latte or a payday or test results from a doctor, waiting is no fun. It can be frustrating, long, and tedious. It requires copious amounts of patience and perseverance. What makes it even more difficult is that we don't live in a society that cultivates patience. Companies compete to offer the fastest service. We have access to fast Internet, fast food, fast delivery, and fast lanes on the freeway. And who doesn't appreciate a fast sermon on Sunday? We can binge-watch every episode of *The Crown* on Netflix at the push of a button. (In my case, several buttons, three remote controls, and my son's help.)

Unlike the conveniences of modern culture, Midnight makes you wait. You wait for your eyes to adjust. You wait for direction. You wait for daylight. Waiting is hard enough when you desire something good, like a meal or a date with a friend. It feels downright cruel when all you want is for your heart to stop aching. You cannot move forward or get out of the place you are in because you are stuck in "not yet" and it's beginning to feel like "not ever." Midnight allows that space inside you to remain when you are desperate to have it filled. Sometimes you don't even know what you are waiting for, but most of the time you do and you just can't get it. You wait for what will ease your pain, whether it is a person, healing, or a change. It's sometimes called the waiting *game*, but it doesn't feel much like a game. It feels like being a worm on a hook. You wriggle and writhe and try to escape, but nothing changes. In Psalm 62, David is waiting too.

> For God alone my soul waits in silence;
>   from him comes my salvation.
> He only is my rock and my salvation,
>   my fortress; I shall not be greatly shaken
> (Psalm 62:1-2 ESV).

David begins Psalm 62 with personal reflections that read like words from a journal. Unlike most of his other songs, David is neither praising God nor lamenting his enemies. He is not singing, thanking, asking, or making a declaration. He's not talking to God's people. He's not even addressing God. Mostly he's murmuring to himself, declaring the state of his own soul. David is alone in his thoughts. All work is finished. All options are exhausted. He isn't worrying, trying, fussing, or really even praying. He's waiting, contrite and vulnerable. Hands open. Heartbroken.

We don't know where David was when he wrote Psalm 62. Was he hiding out in a cave, mercilessly chased by King Saul and his men? Was he already a king writing from his palace? Was he young or old? Had he committed adultery with Bathsheba yet or was that years down the road? No one knows. Whatever the details, David is waiting for God. He is listening for God. Which means God is not talking to him at the moment. God is not telling him to be hopeful or to panic. He's not commanding David or comforting him. God, for the moment, is hiding His face. And David waits.

> How long will all of you attack a man
>> to batter him,
>> like a leaning wall, a tottering fence?
> They only plan to thrust him down from his high position.
>> They take pleasure in falsehood.
> They bless with their mouths,
>> but inwardly they curse (verses 3-4 ESV).

David's situation doesn't sound great. He's battered. He's tottering. It sounds like some pretty nasty people are doing him wrong. We don't know exactly who the people are that David is referring to, but there are plenty of them and they don't sound pleasant. I don't think they'll be receiving a dinner invitation from David anytime soon. Based upon his description, it would be safe to assume David doesn't want them around. Therefore, it would be reasonable for David to pray for those battering, lying, cursing folks to be banished from his life. They are, after all, the source of his problems.

Peculiarly, David isn't focused on them. He isn't fixated on his troubles or how he will get out of them. He is singularly zeroed in on the One who is the source of all comfort, peace, and victory. The psalm begins with "For God alone my soul waits in silence." In Hebrew, it literally means, "Only toward God my soul is silence."[2] For David, there is only one home for his heartache. There is only one place to go: God alone.

This is very unnerving news for those of us who like to rev our engines when things get tough. It is tempting to believe your waiting will be over if you do the right things or participate in the right activities. I mean, surely you can wait *and* still take action, right? Perhaps there is the right Bible study, right prayer, or right church that can help you find your way out of trouble. There must be *something* you can do to get out of this mess. Sometimes that is true, but that is typically when God is waiting for *you*, not the other way around. If David is waiting on God, it means there is no action he can take to move things along. He is not holding any brainstorming sessions with his friends over what he should do next. There are no problem-solving charts in his office. He's not Googling "seven ways to find inner peace" on his computer. His hands are open and empty. His soul is still. He is resigned to wait in silence.

Finding a peaceful place in the midst of Midnight means you will need to learn to wait well. Maybe you will need to act eventually, but now isn't the time. The walls of Midnight are painted in shades of hushed waiting. It is the essence of what you are doing here. If there are gifts to be discovered in this Midnight, and there is something more to this time than just a way to get out of it, then you, like David, will need to wait for God alone. You will need to lean in, quiet your soul, and listen for His still, small voice in the dead of this night.

This is a learned skill. It will take time and concentration and a willingness to feel uncomfortable. Sometimes in life it is difficult to act, but in this case, it will be harder to resist acting. Sitting still and waiting when we just want to run takes immense strength. Waiting on God is an act of submission. It is tremendously vulnerable. It is not for those who are still trusting in their own abilities. It is for those who have exhausted their own strength and are looking for a different way to live. This Midnight is for those who are willing to remain in the complexity of their situation, even when it hurts. We are beloved by God and invited to a David-like relationship with Him. It is an extraordinary opportunity. In *Invitation to Solitude and Silence*, Ruth Haley Barton describes this offering:

> The invitation to solitude and silence is just that. It is an invitation to enter more deeply into the intimacy of relationship with the One who sits just outside the noise and busyness of our lives. It is an invitation to communication and communion with the One who is always present even when our awareness has been dulled by distraction. It is an invitation to the adventure of spiritual transformation in the deepest places of our being, an adventure that will result in greater freedom and authenticity and surrender to God than we have yet experienced.[3]

Right now, when so many options are limited by Midnight, silencing your own soul and waiting for God is still a choice. Busyness is the last bastion of self-protection against overwhelming pain. To willingly stay still in the middle of the pit is an extraordinary act of courage. It takes a lot of chutzpah. David had it. You've got it too.

The Sound of Silence

Have you ever walked into an empty cathedral or church? One with high ceilings, stained glass, pews, and perhaps the slight smell of incense in the air? You look around at the altar, the statues, the hymnals on the back of every pew. Candles unlit. The organ mute.

You cannot help but feel acutely aware of every movement. Each step you take is an echoed intrusion into something sacred. It's quiet, but you can still hear something ethereal and mysterious moving within its walls.

When filming a movie, sound technicians not only record the actors and scenes but also the "room tone." They record action, people, and dialogue, but they also record the sound of the room where the scene took place. When they do this, everyone on the set must remain absolutely still while they capture the, well, "not noise." Essentially, they record nothingness. They turn on their microphones, and for one to two minutes they pick up the sound of the empty room. The air moves differently in different places. Every space has its own ambiance. Recording these tones ensures consistency in the sound of a movie, even when there is nothing to listen to. There are as many variations of quiet as there are to noise.

Midnight has its own sound, the "not noise" of a waiting heart and contrite spirit. It is much like the empty cathedral. Midnight is a quieter time, but it is not without sound and substance. It attunes your ears to the ambient hush of the unknown. It challenges you to quiet your life and mind enough to hear what might be stirring in the midst of the stillness.

Waiting for God alone is an invitation to enter the cathedral of your own soul and discover its contents. You won't know what God will reveal unless you enter this sacred, silent space. You won't even know if God will be there. Until your soul drinks in the sound of silence and waits, still and not searching, contrite yet hopeful, you will not know what David knew. You will not experience what it is to trust in God and His goodness when He seems absent. In this sacred time of stripping away all that is unnecessary, you will need to find a way to embrace silence. It will take time. It will take effort. And it will be unsettling in a thousand different ways. When you wait in the silence for God alone, the possibilities are both intriguing and terrifying.

The Silent God

I've loved words as long as I can remember. I love how they can form stories, poetry, and songs that bring people together. Words have always come easy to me. When I went into ministry, words became even more important, because I used them to speak into other people's lives. I wanted so much for people to learn about God and to use my words to offer His comfort and hope. I felt like I was pretty good at it too. But then there was the day Ken called.

My husband's brother Ken lived about 25 minutes from us and we talked to him every few months. He was a bit on the quiet side and didn't come around often, but we loved it when he would visit or call. Ken was smart, interesting, and had a sweet nature about him. He was single and lived in a small apartment and was a machinist by trade. He kept to himself, but my husband, Danny, and I both felt a particular fondness for Ken because, honestly, he was the easiest, least-complicated relative we knew.

I was just arriving back home from taking the kids out, and when I answered the phone and heard Ken's voice on the line, I was happy to hear from him.

"Hi, Ken!" I said.

"Hi, Melissa. Hey, I wanted to let you know I have some money for you and Danny."

Typically, if I hear someone has money for us, it's an awesome way to start a phone call. But something made my blood run cold when he said those words.

"Ken? What's wrong?"

Silence. Then, "Hey, you probably need to come get it pretty soon, okay?"

"Ken, what are you doing? What are you going to do? Ken?"

"Come soon, okay?"

"Ken, please don't hurt yourself…Please don't. We love you so much. Ken? Ken?"

Silence.

I could hear him breathing on the line and the faint sound of a television, but he said nothing. I dropped to the floor in my living room because my legs couldn't hold me anymore. I lay there on the carpet, sobbing and crying out to God as much as I was crying out to my brother-in-law.

"Ken, I love you. Ken…Ken…"

Oh, God, please help me. Give me the words. Please help me. Tell me what to say.

"Ken?…Are you there?"

It felt like I was running through waist-deep mud, trying to get to Ken but unable to reach him. After a while I didn't hear anything on the line at all. Then I just heard a dial tone. I finally hung up. My husband arrived home right after that, so we got into the car and drove to Ken's apartment. There, we were met by the police. They told us Ken's body was found behind his apartment building. He had shot himself.

I would go over and over that phone call in my mind. In a time of horror and desperate need, the God who changed my life and stirred in me a desire to use words to share His love and grace with others, the God who gave me meaning and peace and who was a constant assurance remained mute when I was on the phone with Ken. During that call, I did not feel His presence or His peace. I did not feel inspired in the words I spoke to Ken. God was silent.

Until that day I had my share of struggles and heartaches, but I had never experienced the utter silence of God. I didn't know what the silence meant. In the days and weeks that followed, I asked

God the question most of us have asked more than once, especially at Midnight: *Why? Why didn't You help me? Why didn't You give me the words? You are the God of the universe and You hold it all in Your hands. I believe it and I know it and You have always been faithful to me. So why were You silent?*

It was a defining moment in my relationship with God, and I grieved. I grieved Ken's anguishing choice. I grieved over the pain he must have felt. I grieved the loss of someone I loved dearly. But I also grieved the loss of the relationship I had with God until this point. In my years of following Him, I always felt His guidance. There were no burning bushes and I never heard Him audibly, but I did experience His steady presence and could always discern His calling. This profound silence added a new dynamic that surprised and baffled me. I couldn't understand why He did not give me the words or the ability to save Ken. Why was I there to answer the phone and yet unable to prevent his death? I grieved that I could no longer hear the Lord's voice or feel His leading. I was ashamed and confused. I didn't know what to think of this new silent God. What had I done to make Him pull away?

Busy Lives, Busy Minds

After Ken died, I spent a long time trying to figure out what it all meant. I went over and over our last conversation, and I came up with about 102 things I should have done differently. Then I took those things and connected them to what I needed to do differently in my relationship with God. I tried to make sense of what happened by using my imagination. I didn't base this on Scripture. I didn't discuss my thoughts with anyone. The entire tragedy left me feeling ashamed and confused, so I kept my imaginings about God and that day to myself. I got really busy stitching together squares of disjointed reasoning, sadness, and shattered illusions and warmed myself with the misshapen quilt they formed. I didn't want to wait for God in silence, because I thought I'd done that already and He was a no-show. When He didn't give me what I thought I needed, I decided staying busy was less painful.

Have you seen those T-shirts that say "Jesus is coming! Look busy!" What do those T-shirts assume about Jesus? That He doesn't like a good nap? Or that He wants us to be scrambling around, panicked and worried about His imminent return? Or are those shirts banking on the reputation that He has in certain circles, the one where He's the angry dad waiting to bust us for smoking cigarettes under the bleachers? Whatever the particulars, the thought that Jesus is coming tempts a lot of us to want to look busy.

We like busy people. Society lauds them. Companies pay them lots of money. Churches put them in charge of barbeques and vacation Bible school. And we like *being* busy people. Doing stuff can make you feel like you matter. If you have a busy calendar, it means you know what's coming. If you are staying active and mapping out your days, you can live in the belief that you are in control.

Busyness is a powerful antidote to helplessness. When you are helpless, it means you are not in control. When you are not in control, it means you might be weak, which means you need someone to help you. This could lead to horrible circumstances, such as bothering someone else with your needs. And that puts you in a place of dependency. And no one likes to be dependent because, let's face it, when you need something, you may or may not get it, which means you might suffer. As we've already established, no one likes to suffer. So you keep going.

Busyness by itself is not bad. Just because your calendar is full doesn't mean there is something wrong with you. Of course, you will find a measure of significance from your job, your relationships, and your calling in life. They were given to you by God and they matter. A lot of the time, you are busy with the things that will not return void, such as Bible studies, prayer, journaling, and church work. They are valuable tools in developing and maturing faith and are important in the life of a believer.

However, when Midnight descends, the things that once gave you comfort, understanding, and brought you closer to God might stop working. Prayers bounce off the ceiling. The words that used to be living and active might now sit flatly on the page of your Bible. When you attend church, surrounded by people, you are dying of loneliness. You search for the God you knew and you cannot find Him using the methods that always worked before.

It's natural to want to understand what God is doing. The problem is that in the desire to understand what is happening, most of us are tempted to make up intricate stories about His motivations. We reflect on the pieces of our story and decide we understand why God has allowed this Midnight and what we must to do to be extricated from it. We put words in His mouth because we would rather find self-comfort with our own small imaginings about His purposes than stop our busy schedule, busy life, and busy mind and wait for Him without understanding His ways.

Silence resides in the darker places of Midnight. It is where our mysterious God often chooses to do His best work. Mother Teresa wrote, "God is a friend of silence. See how nature—trees, flowers, grass—grows in silence; see the stars, the moon and sun, how they move in silence…We need silence to be able to touch our souls."[4] If indeed God is a friend of silence, then we must learn to embrace it as well. It will require effort and vulnerability. It will mean that we stop busying our mind with worries and ideas and all that we imagine God is or is not doing. It will require that we sit for a long time in the deafening "not noise" of the unknown. It is an invitation to the deep places of the soul that only God sees.

But silence is an offer. It's a choice you can make even in the throes of Midnight. You don't need to take it. Just because you are the only person in an empty cathedral doesn't mean you need to sit still. You can shuffle around and murmur to yourself, pick up brochures, leaf through Bibles, and test out the creaky kneelers. You can turn a deaf ear to the invitation and bring your own sound to the space instead. But I hope you won't. It's not the way of Midnight. It wasn't David's way either.

David was a king, which means his calendar was full. He had a large staff, huge armies, and plenty of board meetings and mixers he was obliged to attend, not to mention his burgeoning songwriting career. He had a busy schedule that was filled with people and plans. Despite all his opportunities for distraction, David did not have a busy soul. When he couldn't hear God's voice, he waited for it. When he didn't know what to say to God, he remained silent. When he was in the darkness, he sat still, his soul not yearning for knowledge or peace or resolution but God alone.

In Psalm 62, David ceases activity and stops filling in all the blank spaces in his story with his own imagination about God's motivations. He is waiting for God in the silent unknown stretching out before him. He does not see God. He does not hear Him. And yet David has faith. He doesn't even need to drum it up. No pep talks necessary. In verses 5-7, David repeats himself, but this time he includes what he knows about God as well.

> For God alone, O my soul, wait in silence,
>   for my hope is from him.
> He only is my rock and salvation,
>   my fortress; I shall not be shaken.
> On God rests my salvation and my glory;
>   my mighty rock, my refuge is God (esv).

David allowed his soul to sit in silence. He trusted God so completely that even when he could not hear or feel God, he was sure of His goodness. David most likely sat in silence more than once during his life, because things like that take practice. David had his share of Midnights and they taught him well. He learned how to remain in that fragile, frightening space of the unknown without rushing it, avoiding it, or returning to the noise before it was time. David, through a life of Midnights, found comfort in the elusive, unsettling, and mysterious presence of silence.

The White Space

I took a watercolor painting class last year. On the first night the teacher insisted we get in the habit of leaving at least a little white space in our paintings, that we not fill in every square inch with color. With watercolor, it's the white space that adds dimension, creating a light, translucent effect. She said that white space allows for the observer to fill in the area with their imagination and that it brings the colored parts to life.

Week after week I turned out paintings that looked flat. My teacher said, "You forgot to allow for the white space." Harrumph. I hated white space. I wanted, no, *needed* to fill in every space. I mean it's called painting for a reason, right? She wanted me to leave parts of my paintings blank?

Over time I grudgingly allowed white spaces into my paintings. It took heaps of self-control. Like fruit-of-the-spirit kind of self-control. I had to admit, the white space made my work look better—but it still made me feel uneasy. I was afraid it made the work (*me*) look unfinished, like I messed up or didn't know what I was doing. I enjoyed filling in every space with color. It made me feel less vulnerable, more in control. But it made for boring art.

Silence is like the white space in a watercolor painting. It brings dimension, movement, and mystery to life. It is open to interpretation and leaves room for you to draw your own conclusions, making it one of the more vulnerable experiences we can have. But vulnerability is the beginning of intimacy, and intimacy is the heart of a deep relationship. To sit quietly in the same room with another person without needing to talk or act is a sign of deep connectedness. You wouldn't be alone in a room with an acquaintance without saying anything. One of you would feel the urge to make small talk or at least acknowledge the other's presence. Vulnerable, intimate silence is safe only with those to whom you are closest. Vulnerable silence is sitting side-by-side with a friend at the hospital while you both read outdated magazines and wait for the doctor. It's the consecrated moments between a husband and wife before they drift off to sleep. Vulnerable silence is when your teenager is inexplicably crying her eyes out and all you can do is hold her until she falls asleep in your lap.

I attended a Catholic Mass a while ago, and when it was time for the priest to give the homily, he eased out of his chair, stood up, and said, "Last night, Tom and Marie's five-day-old son died. They are with us this morning. There are no words. I have nothing more to say today." No one made a sound as he made his way over to the altar to continue with the service. It was the most powerful sermon I've ever heard. It was four sentences. Father McNamara honored those grieving parents with his silence. The congregation did the same. There is a reason we mark so many tragedies in our nation with a moment of silence. Sometimes words fall short.

Words don't need to fill up all the spaces, especially in deep relationships. There is such knowing, understanding, and deep trust that we can allow silence to enter and it will not be a threat. We can be content in the quiet of one another's company. As a matter of fact, it draws us closer because anything more than silence would steal something from those sacred moments.

God's silence doesn't imply His indifference. Stillness is not the same as stagnation. White space is not the same as blank space. Perhaps the Lord is honoring your grief. Maybe He is grieved too. You can trust there is as much going on in the white space of God's silence as there is in the color of what you see. Silence creates beauty that might not look too splashy by itself, but it makes everything around it more beautiful. It makes things come alive. Silence gives your Midnight depth and dimension. It honors what is happening in this sacred, painful time. Silence, like the white space in a watercolor, will draw your attention to what needs to be focused on.

Moreover, in leaving the white spaces in your life, God is being vulnerable with *you*. He opens Himself up to have things assumed about Him that are inaccurate. He is risking that you will take the white space and believe the worst about Him. In this time of silence, you have the option to draw your own conclusions about God, to feel He is doing or not doing certain things, that His plan is terrible or amazing, cruel or a blessing. God's offer of silent white spaces is His invitation to intimacy, to sit side by side with Him and allow His mystery into the most vulnerable places of your soul. He is reaching out His hand in the midst of the darkness and asking you to trust Him without knowing the plan, to believe without seeing the future. He is inviting you to trust His goodness and grace in the midst of unbearable pain. You can turn away. You can get busy filling in all the white space. You can assume He is cruel and forgo a relationship with Him altogether. Or you, like David, can sit in stillness before the Lord. You can allow this terrifying, beautiful silence to settle deep into your soul and trust all you do not understand. Vulnerability with Him is always better than control without Him.

These unknown expanses are not blank places where God has left us alone, they are the white spaces in this masterpiece. Mysterious and beautiful, they make our life with Him far more complex and intimate. The Creator is making something exquisite, and silence is part of His work in us.

Quieted

It's been over ten years since Ken's suicide. It will never be okay with me, and I will never know why God allowed it. Our family still grieves. But my soul has been quieted by Ken's death. The silence has allowed room for grief and for the process of learning new things about the deeper ways of God. I no longer fear silence and stillness, and I've stopped believing they mean the absence of something good.

Silence has allowed me the freedom in ministry not to have all the answers. I find myself responding to people's questions about God and why He does and doesn't do things with "I don't know" much more often than before. I don't want to minimize people's grief or pain with a bunch of flat, meaningless words. Sometimes silence is the best thing we can give, especially when accompanied by our presence.

The longest silence recorded in Scripture is the 400 years between the book of Malachi in the Old Testament and the birth of Jesus Christ in the New. But God told the Israelites long before then, "I will never leave you nor forsake you" (Joshua 1:5). If you have put your faith in Jesus Christ, God's silence never means His absence.

The Lord denied my desire for His voice in that moment with Ken, and He denied me the ability to save Ken with my words. But God has never, even for a moment, denied His presence. He was there with me on the carpet that day. He is with you too. He offers His silence—sacred, hushed, and accompanied by His holy and loving presence—even when you don't feel it. You can learn to embrace quiet and to trust God's silence as deeply as you have trusted His voice.

The Gift of Silence

> It is a blessed mark of growth out of spiritual infancy when we can forgo the joys which once appeared to be essential, and can find our solace in Him who denies them to us.
>
> —C.H. Spurgeon[5]

The message of the gospel is that there is nothing you can do to make God love you more than He does in this very moment. Because Jesus made atonement for us on the cross, there is nothing we can do to separate us from His love. But it goes against our human nature to trust such a thing. We like to work for our rewards. We like to sing for our supper because it makes us feel like we are in control. The painful, scary truth of our life is that we do not have control.

The gift of silence allows you to embrace your powerlessness. It is a practice of both the mind and the body that invites the unknown. It is an invitation to surrender all of the ways you try to control your life with noise and busyness. Sometimes the best way for you to let go of the control you never really had is to stop everything and let silence fill the space.

The gift of silence is that it serves as an important passage to deep David-like communion with God. It will take practice to stay still. Everything in you will want to get busy, figure out God's plans, or grasp at control. Don't relent. If you are never completely quieted before God, how will you know in the deepest part of your soul that you are loved by Him with an everlasting love? How will you learn that His love is higher and wider and deeper and longer than you can see when you keep trying to paint in all the white space with your actions? Maybe, like David, this Midnight is calling you to sit in silence and wait for God alone. No work. No prayer. No reading. No fasting. No worship music. No scripture cards. Just you. Sitting. Waiting. Silent.

I am not suggesting that you put your Bible away and give up prayer forever. But perhaps you can do it for a while, just for this special time, when Jesus is calling you to a greater intimacy with Him. It's probably antithetical to everything you think you need to do to get out of your pain. It could be, but I don't think so. Reread the first two verses of Psalm 62 (ESV): "For God alone my soul waits in silence; from him comes my salvation. He alone is my rock and my salvation, my fortress; I shall not be greatly shaken." David, the man who penned more songs to God than anyone…David, the boy with the faith to take down a giant…David, the conqueror, the king, the lover of God, set down his musical instruments and sacred books in his Midnight. He ceased prayer and petition and allowed the silence to settle into his soul. He did what only the most faithful can do when all else fails. He did nothing.

I hesitated to write about Ken because it is so deeply personal and still hurts so much. But then I read David's instruction at the beginning of Psalm 62: "For the director of music. For Jeduthan." Jeduthan was one of David's favorite worship leaders. He was like the Chris Tomlin of David's time. I don't know if he made CDs available in the lobby of the temple, but I'm sure they would have sold like hotcakes. David took the innermost thoughts of his heart and made them into a worship song for others. He didn't keep this lament to himself but made it available for each of us to proclaim. He shared his deepest reflections so we can know that we are not alone. We, too, can find intimacy with God in the unknown.

David's transparency gave me the courage to do the same. Everyone will be faced with a Midnight, but not everyone will sit in silence and wait for God. Hands open. Heartbroken. David wants us to know it is always an option.

> Trust in him at all times, O people;
>> pour out your heart before him;
>> God is a refuge for us (Psalm 62:8 ESV).

The gift of silence is that it reflects the mystery of God. It is the white space of trust. Silence is necessary in order to develop a faith that is not dependent upon word or action or feeling. It is the path to submission before God. The longer you sit in stillness before the Lord, the more you will become comfortable with the quieter places of Midnight. You won't need to fill in the silence with your own assumptions about what God is doing, because your faith will allow for mystery. Contentment will embrace the unknown in the hushed cathedral of Midnight. The "not noise" of silence will be a warm blanket around your shoulders and your soul will be stilled. The grace of God's silence is that you can trust it as much as you can trust His voice. Like David, you will discover a life of deep faith in God that transcends words. You will know that even when He does not speak, He is still there, doing His sacred, sanctified, Midnight work.

MOONLIGHT MEDITATIONS

- Where in your Midnight do you long to hear God speak?
- What measures do you take to avoid silence?
- What areas in your life do you need to simply do nothing in this Midnight?

EVENING STROLL

- Find a comfortable space, quiet your mind, and concentrate on the words of Psalm 62:1-2 (ESV) and the prayers that follow. Say them aloud. Allow them to become your words too.

For God alone my soul waits...

I will wait for You, God. You alone make me safe and secure. You alone are the source of my wholeness and healing. You alone are my peace and perseverance. I will rely upon You, God. Though I cannot see You, I will believe in Your presence. Even when You are silent, I will trust in Your goodness.

in silence;

I will embrace Your mystery with confidence. I will trust Your ways that are so different than mine. I can let go of the safety of noise and busyness. I will lean in to the sound of silence. I will listen to the "not noise." I do not need to be afraid of what I will hear.

from him comes my salvation.

Because of Your love, God, I don't need to take any action. I don't need to do more. I don't need to act more. I don't need to be more than I already am at this moment. I don't need to be out of this Midnight, because You are with me in it. I can put down my weapons and drop my armor. My soul is quiet and contrite before You.

He alone is my rock and my salvation,

I will trust Your purposes even when I don't understand them. Even when they break my heart. I will trust that You are working even when I don't see it. I know that Your plan for my life is not blank even when I am surrounded by white space.

my fortress;

Because of Your faithfulness, I am safe within the mist of the unknown. You are present even when You are silent. You do not leave or forsake Your children. Ever.

I shall not be greatly shaken.

I can sit in the silence, waiting for You. You are invited into the quiet cathedral of my soul. I will draw near to You as You draw near to me. In this Midnight, You are closer than ever. You will not let me go. Amen.

GARBO, LONELINESS, AND THE UNWAVERING GAZE OF GRACE

Solitude is different from loneliness, and it doesn't have to be a lonely kind of thing.

MISTER ROGERS[1]

Since Midnight isn't the best place to begin new projects, take on more responsibility, or attend parties that require uncomfortable shoes, it's tempting to avoid all contact with the outside world until you feel fun and interesting again. You don't feel comfortable in your own skin, so why would you feel at ease with others? It's easier to sit out the social scene and wait for Midnight to pass. Not exactly a great plan, but an understandable one.

Greta Garbo was a film star in both silent movies and some of the first talkies. In the movie *Grand Hotel*, she uttered one of the most famous movie lines in all of movie history: "I want to be alone."[2] It became synonymous with the actress herself. Though it was originally written for a script, it was representative of Garbo's personal mystique. She was notoriously private and spent a lot of her free time alone. Garbo was never comfortable with her fame and was mystified that people were curious about her private life.[3] She was an actress. It was her job. Why did anyone care who she dated or where she vacationed? If she were alive today, I doubt she'd be posting online photos of the tuna sandwich she ate for lunch.

But the quote that became so closely associated with her did not reflect her true feelings. Later in her life she emphasized, "I never said I want to be alone. I only said I want to be let alone. There is all the difference."[4] Like Garbo, I find tremendous peace in being alone. It feels like wide-open space to me. It's where I can be free of expectations and pesky things like answering questions, maintaining manners, and wearing a bra. A bit of intentional distance from the world can be revitalizing. I think that's the distinction Garbo was making. She didn't want to be marooned on a desert island; she just needed a little space.

Slowing down in the midst of Midnight can be a gift, a respite from a busy schedule, a busy mind, and a busy world. Sometimes alone is the best place to be. There is a certain thrill to turning down invitations and staying home in your pajamas. It indicates an internal freedom. And yet the opposite can be just as true. At times you might stay distant because you have lost the choice to do anything else. The very idea of getting dressed, leaving the house, and actually talking to others is absolutely overwhelming. When you are afraid to go out, afraid of people, afraid of telling anyone what is happening for fear of rejection, that's not freedom—it's slavery. I've worn those rusted chains so often I'm pretty sure I've got tetanus. There is a big difference between the solitude that feeds your soul and the isolation that leads to starvation.

Solitude vs. Isolation

Midnight is a lonely experience for three reasons.

First, no one will understand exactly what you are going through, because it's your journey alone. This is painful and frustrating. When you attempt to put your experience into words, you'll worry that you sound unhinged. It's disconcerting for everyone involved. The only alternative is removing yourself from close contact. It's like when a bone is first broken. Before you get a cast put on, you don't want anyone to accidentally touch it, because the pain would be excruciating. It's the same for your heart. Since it's difficult for those you love to understand what is happening, sometimes it is easier to wrap your brokenness in a plaster cast of loneliness to avoid being hurt.

Second, it's exhausting. Pain, emotional or physical, wears a person out. The instinct to be alone is an act of self-preservation. Midnight can feel like a marathon, and all your energy goes toward just taking the next step. You don't have any energy to spare. Also, people in general are nuts. I say that in the most Christian way possible. But they are, and they make me tired. I like to be in my own company because, although I'm nuts too, my brand of nuttiness makes sense to me. It's not as exhausting. I like to think of it as winsome and eccentric. I'm unsure my husband would describe it in the same way, but I know enough not to inquire. A happy marriage is built on discerning which questions should remain unasked.

Third, no one wants to look like a hot mess. Sometimes I worry that if I am a wreck in front of others, I might not be a good Christian witness. Like I'm bad advertising. I know in my head that this reasoning goes against the entire reason we trust Jesus in the first place. Nonetheless, if I'm honest, it's a concern. To be even more honest, it's not my main concern. My main motivation for being alone when I'm hurting is that I care deeply about what people think of me. I want people to like me. Call it vanity. Call it pride. Call it codependence. But that's the truth. I really want people to like me, and I'm afraid my struggles will turn them away. I'm terrified I will be simultaneously too much and not enough for my friends and family. If I actually told them everything that goes on in my mind and shared all the ways I feel afraid and ashamed, they might turn away once and for all. Then I really would be by myself.

It's ironic. We often keep to ourselves because we are terrified of being alone. Abandonment is our deepest fear, and yet the fear of it can create our deepest loneliness. We don't share the full truth about ourselves with others because we are afraid of people, of rejection, of all the emotions that swirl around in our head. We don't talk about how ashamed we are, because if we speak it, we might feel more shame. We will expose all the ways we are inadequate and ill-equipped for this world. Many of us feel like an adolescent trying to make his or her way in a grown-up world. We feel embarrassed that we cannot properly manage the onslaught of challenges each day brings. We assume we lack something others possess. We live with a sense of missing something profound and important and vital to our personhood, something others have. We feel like we are failing at life. In our embarrassment, we keep pretending we've got it together. This only adds to our loneliness. Every fear, every vulnerability, every wound we wrap up and hide deep inside ourselves is another brick between us and everyone else. If we keep living this way, we will be so barricaded from the world that we will end up in desolate isolation. This is not solitude. This is a place so lonely and black that it is not even a Midnight. There are no stars. There is no moon. This is a place without rhythm or beauty or gifts. Isolation that bleak is a hellish existence. If you are in that place, you are in a fight for your life.

Deep Thirst, Deeper Quenching

> You, God, are my God,
>   earnestly I seek you;

I thirst for you,
  my whole being longs for you,
in a dry and parched land
  where there is no water (Psalm 63:1).

David starts Psalm 63 with desperate longing, deep and imbued with agony. David is alone in a parched land. Whether it's physical or psychological, we don't know. It doesn't make a whit of a difference though, does it? He is crying out for communion, a place away from the wasteland of loneliness. David is searching for relief, and he goes to the first place he knows to find it. "You, God, are my God, earnestly I seek you."

One of the benefits of Midnight is that it naturally makes us desperate. This can be a good thing when it motivates us to find relief in healthy ways. It's not pretty, but it focuses our attention. It can make us desperate enough to reach out for God. It can serve as the commencement of a deeper relationship with the Lord. Pursuing God is one of the most life-changing actions we can take. If desperation is what gets us moving in that direction, that's okay. At least we are moving.

When you are in the middle of a really dark season, I know the last thing you might feel like doing is pursuing anything. You want to talk neither with God nor anyone else about the depth of your sadness. Maybe you're ashamed or overwhelmed or you're not even sure where to begin. Perhaps you're afraid you will scare people away from you. That is a really hard, lonely place to be. But the longer you stay in isolation, the more vulnerable you are to untrue, untethered thinking.

Remember that guy in the basement? The one who leans in real close and whispers accusations and judgments? When you are alone, he will tell you it's always been this awful and will always be this awful. He will tell you there is no hope. He will say you have much to be ashamed of. He knows just enough about your life to make you feel small and powerless. But he's a liar. He wants to get you alone so no one is there to contradict him. Despite his authoritative tone and deeply personal attacks, he is not in charge of this Midnight. If the guy in the basement is leaning in close to you right now, and you are sliding into desperation, it's time to be alone with someone else besides him.

Just because you are going through a difficult time, it doesn't necessarily mean that you've got a diagnosable, long-term mental illness. Struggle is part of the human experience. But sometimes grief, depression, or deep suffering needs the attention of a professional. These people are trained in dealing with the guy in the basement. They know his tricks. They also can help you begin to put words to all you are thinking and feeling. They know what questions to ask and how to get to the root of your sadness. They will be able to help release you from suffocating shame and self-loathing. If you feel worthless, hopeless, or lost, counseling can be a life-changing experience.

For me, the most significant result of going to counseling was that when I shared my deepest, most shameful thoughts, feelings, and experiences, my therapist didn't leave the room. He stayed put. He didn't furrow his brows or clutch his chest in horror at my revelations. He didn't wag his finger at me or give me a judgmental "tsk! tsk!" He didn't laugh. He didn't kick me out of his office. He was attentive, compassionate, and present. He sat and listened and he didn't leave. It was astonishing.

When I started to speak about the things the guy in the basement told me were unspeakable, shame loosened its grip on me. When my counselor listened without judgment, I started to feel less judgmental about my own issues. When he didn't shame me, I began to feel less ashamed. The experience profoundly impacted my relationship with God.

After sharing with my counselor week in and week out for some time, it occurred to me that if he didn't run screaming out of the room when I shared my innermost secrets, God might not be doing that either. I understood God's love in theory, but having an actual person sit with me and listen with kindness to all the things I've been most ashamed of made the grace of God a real experience. I could imagine it more clearly. If another human being, imperfect and flawed with his own problems, could stay with me in my worst moments, then God is more than capable of doing the same thing. I wasn't so isolated anymore. Counseling was my first taste of true solitude, because it taught me the soul-quenching gift of being alone in the presence of grace.

Midnight can be lonely, but it never should lead to isolation. There are resources that can help: exercise, therapy, rest, medication. These are good, God-given tools that provide for your body and mind. You are not separate from these aspects of your personhood. Midnight encompasses the physical, mental, and spiritual facets of your being. Pay attention to what your body is telling you and seek out ways to care for it well. Be alert for thinking that is hopeless, self-harming, or life-threatening. Depression might even be a secondary reaction to a physical malady. Find a good doctor who can be an advocate, one who will be with you and help identify what your body and brain need. Find a counselor to walk with you in this process. And allow their care to remind you that you have a God who cares deeply for your mind, body, and soul as well. You are worthy of compassion and kindness. You are worthy of support. You are worthy of the effort it will take to ask for help.

Solitude is imperative to the transforming work of Midnight.

But it is not simply time alone. It's not "me time" or a way to protect yourself from the nutty people of the world. It is not meant to protect your heart or your pride by embracing isolation. In good times, it will be a natural outpouring of joy. In desperate times, you might enter into solitude with a cry like David's: "My God, my God, earnestly I seek you." Solitude is the intentional, personal seeking out of God done in the deepest places of your heart and mind. Solitude, like silence, is vulnerable, but it is decidedly more active. It is the pursuit of dedicated time in the company of your Creator. Solitude is an invitation to savor God's presence. It is the act of becoming available to Him who is right there with you. Time alone with another person (like a counselor) can be a wonderful first step away from the agony of isolation and toward the richness of solitude with God. C.S. Lewis wrote, "Look for yourself, and you will find in the long run only hatred, loneliness, despair, rage, ruin, and decay. But look for Christ, and you will find Him, and with Him everything else thrown in."[5]

Even if you have a good counselor or doctor, your soul longs for its Creator. When David was in a parched and weary place, he knew God alone could quench his innermost thirst. David knew what is true about you as well, that you have a God who is full of compassion and grace and loves you completely. No matter what you think, say, do, or feel, He never leaves the room. Solitude is turning your attention to His presence.

Turning Focus

Ahhh…bedtime. When all the tasks are done and it's time to rest. When the troubles of the day drift off into a fitful, long sleep. When cares are released and peace sets in. Yeah, *right*.

Just as the lights go out and my head hits the pillow, when I am ready to release all of the stimulation, frustration, and distractions of the day, my brain calls an all-skate. It's like when I'd go to the roller rink as a kid, and the DJ would invite everyone, from novice to expert, onto the floor at the same time. Every neurotic thought and feeling rolls onto the rink of my mind, bumping and pushing into one another. Some are inching forward, holding on to the walls for dear life. Other thoughts gain momentum with each passing second. Some ideas skate backwards. A lot of the feelings do flips. Some hold hands with other thoughts like a couple on their first date. They all trip over one another. My DJ brain has called out an all-skate every night for as long as I can remember. Sometimes I can faintly hear the song "Gloria" by Laura Branigan playing as my worries swoosh by.

Nothing can bring on anxiety more than meandering through your problems without purpose or direction. But solitude is not untethered rumination. Nor is it an emptying of your mind. That would be as fruitless as it would be difficult. Your brain is always at work. As Aristotle said, "Nature abhors a vacuum."[6] Our minds naturally fill space.

Cultivating solitude is the practice of turning your focus away from your worries, feelings, and circumstances and toward the living God. It is to intentionally enter into His presence. It is to seek Him out in the midst of the chaos of body and mind. It is a regular practice. It doesn't come naturally; it's a muscle that needs to be developed. It is not your job to make God show up. He's already with you. Solitude is the conduit to an *awareness* of His presence.

Solitude requires being intentional with your time. It will not fall into your lap. There will be all kinds of distractions to pull you away. It will require trial and error. It will feel weird. You will need to get comfortable with silence. But if you continue to practice it, you will find more light in the darkness than you ever thought possible. Solitude helps you to unearth the radiance of Midnight. And it takes practice.

Practicing Solitude

To practice solitude, find a comfortable space to be by yourself. It can be in your home, your car, indoors, or outside. But it must be a place where you will have few interruptions and not a lot of noise. Sometimes I set a timer so I won't be worried that I will forget to pick up the kids from school or take the chicken out of the oven. Twenty minutes is a long time to sit still when it's not part of your routine. Come to think of it, have you ever made microwave popcorn? Even two minutes can feel like a long time. Maybe just set the timer for two minutes at first. Then go up to three and four minutes and so on as you are ready.

If it helps, you can close your eyes. Breathe in, breathe out, and embrace what it feels like to be in your own skin. Note where your mind is naturally going—toward the worries of the day, your next meal, or the hair appointment you need to make. It's fine to think about those things, but not right now. Those things will keep. Stay quiet. Allow yourself to simply be in this mental and physical space. Lean in to the sound of silence. It's time to gently turn your attention toward God. Offer this time to Him. Confess your hesitation. Thank Him for His presence. He is always there, even when you cannot feel Him. Ask Him to reveal Himself to you in ways that are both personal and practical. With the best of your ability, stay focused on Him.

As you try to concentrate on God, you will immediately begin wondering, *Is this it? Am I doing this right? Is something supposed to happen?* You will wonder if you are messing it up somehow. How will you know if you are doing it right? Matthew 7:7-8 says, "Ask and it will be given to you; seek and you will find; knock and the door will be opened to you. For everyone who asks receives; the one who seeks finds; and to the one who knocks, the door will be opened." Jesus will not keep the door shut. His entire plan, from the beginning of time, was to bring you to Himself. When you focus on Jesus, your soul remembers its purpose. You're made to be transformed by the presence of God. You are created to enjoy being with Him.

Now, a big fiery bush will most likely not appear in your backyard. It's doubtful the angel Gabriel will show up with an announcement. I'm not saying you will hear audibly from God in a voice sounding eerily like Morgan Freeman. You probably won't. If you are waiting for something supernatural and sweeping to happen, you might be waiting for quite a while. On the whole, solitude is more subtle than that. But I promise you this: God did not send His Son into the world to die on a cross and rise again from the dead and then promise the Holy Spirit just to leave you to your own devices. He will make Himself known.

It's totally normal if your mind wanders all over the place. At one moment you might be praying and in the next you're making out your grocery list. No big deal. Just refocus your attention on God and leave the groceries for later. Don't beat yourself up if you can't focus for more than a couple of minutes. The longer you practice solitude, the longer you will be able to sit in the stillness without jumping out of your skin. I usually keep a pad of paper near me. If I suddenly remember something I don't want to forget, I can quickly write it down. It allows me to get back to the business at hand a lot faster than trying to practice solitude *and* not forget to pay the water bill. A lot of times, I journal. It helps keep my mind focused. Remember, it's not about results; it's about focusing on what or rather Who is already with you. It's an act of worship.

Sometimes solitude goes awry. Even when you have the best intentions, you can't control everything going on around you. Sometimes it will seem like the world is conspiring against you, preventing your solitude with God. This is normal. It is why you need to make a regular practice of solitude. It won't always go the way you'd expect.

This is a page of my journal on one of the days I tried (note: *tried*) to stay focused on time with the Lord.

> *September 8*
>
> So much of me wants to seek out solitude and silence but it seems like everything around me wants just the opposite. Flies buzz in my ears and the dog whines for attention and the television is loud. It plays a show I'm not sure Elizabeth should be watching and I debate if I'm doing the Lord's work best by ignoring it and doggedly try to find a place of silence or if I should more closely monitor the things that influence her, which means I should get up and suggest the Disney channel instead. Danny tromps through the bedroom and into the bathroom where he clatters about. He announces we are out of Q-tips. The dog sees the cat and bolts from my side, which startles and irritates me. Danny turns the shower on and the sound of the water beats into my temples and I feel exasperated resentment begin to take hold of the very heart that simply wanted to spend time with You.
>
> [Later that same day] I decided to sit outside in a park where the weather is beautiful. There was a homeless couple nearby which gave me pause, immediately followed by self-chastisement. "Don't be so paranoid, Melissa. They are harmless. These people are the people Jesus loves. It's daylight. Don't be a weirdo."
>
> I walk two steps more and a questionable-looking man comments that I am very pretty and makes a whirling sound. He seems harmless. He saunters by. I fight the urge to go back to my car and lock the doors. I want to enjoy silence and communion with God, but

I also want to feel the sun on my face and feel the wind and enjoy the shade of a tree and be out among God's people. I don't want to be afraid. I don't want to relegate my quiet time to the car—windows rolled up, door locked, parked along a random street where the lawns are tightly manicured.

Said questionable-looking man now does an about-face, walks back in my direction, and plops himself down next to me on the park bench. He tells me it was too pretty of a day to get high all by himself at home. He goes further to tell me about the wine he's got in his black plastic bag. He pulls out a cigarette and matches but doesn't light up. He puts his hand out and introduces himself and I shake his hand and tell him my name. His hands are smooth and clean.

He mentions that he is waiting for the bus and looks at his watch. When he declares the time, I realize it's been 15 minutes since I left my car and my only prayer has been *"Oh, God, please don't let me get murdered."* And it's been anything but silent. In addition to conversation with my new friend, cars whiz by. Ambulance sirens blare. A train blasts its horn long and loud.

I am not sure what to do now. Do I retreat to my car? If so, why would I be doing that? Am I afraid of being alone in the park or am I really seeking a time of silence? I don't want to offend my new bench-mate, and yet I'm incredibly aware that there has been more than one victim of crime who ended up that way because they didn't want to offend anyone.

Note: Just as I'm wondering if this journal entry will be my last, he gets up and runs toward the approaching bus. He turns back, waves kindly, and smiles at me. "Good-bye, beautiful!" I can't help but smile. Oh, gosh, the homeless couple is heading over with their pit bull, of all things. I'd better go.

Solitude is trial and error. And yet, when I reflect on my journal entry, I can see that it was a sacred day unto itself. It wasn't what I wanted out of the solitude and certainly not what I expected. But God showed up. Isn't that the point of seeking Him? Solitude may not garner immediate results. But the habit alone will deepen your relationship with God. Not because the angels will weep every time you seek Him, but because the seeking itself reorients your heart toward Him. Because it is a practice, it's something you will need to return to again and again. There is no magic formula. Your experience will be your own. You might feel ridiculous at first. You might feel scared. You might get frustrated that you are pulled in 17 directions the moment you try to carve out any time with God. Persevere. Don't let the voice of condemnation, perfectionism, or criticism steal the time away. That voice is not from God. Turn your attention away from worry and fear. I know it's much easier said than done. But it's worth it.

Digging in Your Heels

If you are overwhelmed at the prospect of having to work for solitude, keep in mind that worrying requires effort too. It might come more naturally, but it is still a matter of attention and energy. Romans 12:2 encapsulates this idea well. I especially like The Message translation: "Don't become so well-adjusted to your culture that you fit into it without even thinking. Instead, fix your attention on God. You'll be changed from the inside out. Readily recognize what he wants from you, and quickly respond to it. Unlike the culture around you, always dragging you down to its level of immaturity, God brings the best out of you, develops well-formed maturity in you."

Your culture begins with your mind. Your thoughts are powerful. They direct your attentions. They tell you where to look and what to focus on. When Paul told the Corinthians, "We take captive every thought" (2 Corinthians 10:5), he wasn't merely saying, "Don't think about the bad stuff." He was saying that when the ideas and thoughts that weigh down your soul arise, compare them to the truth of what Jesus says. If they don't line up, then you have another, better, truer place to bring your thoughts.

In Psalm 63, David begins with a desperate cry to God. In the next few verses, he does an about-face. He leaves behind his descriptions of barren and parched places. He focuses on the Lord. He turns his attention on the God who has been with him before and is with him in his present pain.

> I have seen you in the sanctuary
>> and beheld your power and your glory.
> Because your love is better than life,
>> my lips will glorify you.
> I will praise you as long as I live,
>> and in your name I will lift up my hands.
> I will be fully satisfied as with the richest of foods;
>> with singing lips my mouth will praise you.
> On my bed I remember you;
>> I think of you through the watches of the night.
> Because you are my help,
>> I sing in the shadow of your wings.
> I cling to you;
>> your right hand upholds me (verses 2-8).

This is where David's stubborn streak shows up. David had a friendship with God. He knew God's character. He'd been witness to God's faithfulness and power throughout the years. While he might not have been experiencing it all in that moment, he could draw on his memory. He shifted his thoughts from desperation to God's faithful abundance. He dug in his heels and focused on what he knew to be true. He *willed* his thoughts to be directed toward God.

My lips *will* glorify you.

I *will* praise you.

I *will* lift up my hands.

I *will* be fully satisfied.

I *remember* you.

I *think* of you.

I *cling* to you.

David refused to let the dry and weary land parch his soul. He decided to take the all-skate in his head and make it form a single line, rolling right to God. I am not saying you need to ignore all your concerns and just "stay positive." You don't need to paint a smile on your face or pretend you are not suffering when you are. Besides, who can do that for very long? Being fake takes a lot of energy. To orient your pain toward God is to find satisfaction for your deeper needs. The direction of your mind will radically shift your experience of Midnight.

Maybe the act of concentrating on anything is too much for you. Practicing solitude is not meant to produce shame or guilt or feelings of failure. Sometimes you're not up for much of anything. Sometimes all you can do is groan. What I am asking you to do is groan in His direction. In the final three verses of Psalm 63, David writes:

> Those who want to kill me will be destroyed;
>   they will go down to the depths of the earth.
> They will be given over to the sword
>   and become food for jackals.
> But the king will rejoice in God;
>   all who swear by God will glory in him,
>   while the mouths of liars will be silenced (verses 9-11).

David is reminding himself who is boss. He's speaking the underlying truth to his overwhelming feelings.

The voice in your head that insists you are alone in this world is your enemy. It wants to destroy you. It is trying desperately to pull you down into the depths of the earth. But you cannot be dragged out of the company of Jesus. His territory doesn't have boundary lines. Neither does His love for you. Even in this Midnight, you can rejoice in God. It may not be "hands waving in the air" kind of rejoicing, but it can be rejoicing nonetheless. When directing your heart and mind toward God, the mouths of the liars, the accusers, the ones who insist you are alone will be shut.

Suffering experienced in isolation is hell. But in the company of Jesus Christ, it is sanctification. He is with you, He is your help, and His right hand is upholding you. Like David, the truest thing about you is that you are fervently loved by God. You can rejoice in His presence.

The Gift of Solitude

> A spiritual kingdom lies all about us, enclosing us, embracing us, altogether within reach of our inner selves, waiting for us to recognize it. God Himself is here waiting for our response to His presence. This eternal world will come alive to us the moment we begin to reckon upon its reality.
>
> —A. W. Tozer[7]

Midnight will bring you to your knees. Maybe your first inclination is to hurry up and rise. But I hope you don't. Solitude is a sacred opportunity to draw closer to God and to discover His true nature. It's thirst that motivates us to find water. The dry and weary land is the backdrop to full satisfaction in Christ.

The gift of solitude is that it trains your mind to look for Christ in the midst of pain. It is the seat of transformation. Over time and with practice, your mind will more quickly turn from desolation to abundance. Distractions and worries will have less control over you because you are in the habit of groaning in His direction.

Of all the gifts of Midnight, solitude is the most tangible. It engages both your physical body and your mind. It quiets your surroundings and your heart. It is for all seasons, at all times. Solitude is for daytime and night. It is for chill and warmth. It is for times of desperation and times of abundance. It is the gift that will stay with you even after the Midnight recedes.

Solitude offers a place where the chaos cannot go. It is a pool of living water in the middle of a dry and weary land. It is where you will come to understand that your depression, your pain, your suffering will not have the last word. You can dig your heels in, get stubborn, and orient yourself toward Christ. Solitude is a place of grit as much as grace.

When you focus your attention on the God who holds you dear, you will discover a love that is better, stronger, and more satisfying than anything else in life. It doesn't mean that you will skip through the tulips every day. Sometimes it will be a trudge in the desert. But tulips or sand, God is present. To spend time in solitude with God is to behold His power and glory. It is to trust that when you focus your attention on Him, you'll experience His loving attention toward you.

The deepest pain we can know is utter aloneness. It is more damaging than any physical pain because there is no one to share our burden. It is born out of the idea that no one truly understands the complexity of our thoughts, wounds, and journey. It is confirmed by how exhausting it is to be around others. The fear of being misunderstood or ashamed keeps us in chains. Isolation is solitary confinement for our soul.

Solitude is the opposite of solitary confinement because it unlocks the prison of aloneness. It moves past bone and marrow and roots itself down deep, allowing us to know and be known by our Creator. It brings us into communion with Christ. It is the place to understand deep in our soul that we are not alone in our pain— ever. It is the practice of looking around long enough to discover Abba, who has been with us all along. In *Celebration of Discipline*, Richard Foster writes,

> If we possess inward solitude we do not fear being alone, for we know that we are not alone. Neither do we fear being with others, for they do not control us. In the midst of the noise and confusion we are settled into a deep inner silence. Whether alone or among people, we always carry with us a portable sanctuary of the heart.[8]

Because of Jesus Christ, there is no more separation between you and God. You can approach His throne of grace in confidence. He is with you in the watches of the night. You can rest safe in the shadow of His wings. You will be richly satisfied with nothing less than Jesus Christ Himself. The gift of solitude is that as you experience the soul-deep acceptance of God, you will be able to make peace with this Midnight. The journey of shame can end. To stand in the presence of God is to stand in the presence of goodness and mercy. It is a place of transformation and sanctification.

The gift of solitude is that in searching and finding God, you will find your truest self. You have been fashioned in His image and you are beloved by Him at all times, in all places, in the light of day, and in the dark of Midnight. The essence of who you are lies within His unwavering gaze of affection and grace.

MOONLIGHT MEDITATIONS

- What parts of Midnight are loneliest for you?

- Have you been spending time alone in order to rest and find renewal or are you isolated from God and others?

- When you practice solitude, what questions or insecurities arise?

- How can solitude be beneficial in your Midnight?

- What ideas do you have to ensure more intentional time alone with God?

EVENING STROLL

- Make an appointment with your physician. Explain what you are experiencing. Be as honest and detailed as possible. Get a physical exam. This will help to ensure there is not a physical condition contributing to your emotional pain. Medication might be a helpful component to healing your brain, your body, or both.

- Consider your thoughts in this time. Are they leading you toward hopelessness or self-harm? Are you currently in the parched land of isolation? If so, it's time to get professional, experienced help. Even if you are not feeling desperate, extra support and care through counseling is a wonderful option. Let the experience of being alone with another person who offers compassion and grace point you toward the God who offers the truest rest for your soul.

- Read over the first part of the "Practicing Solitude" section in this chapter. Put the suggestions into action. As

often as possible, set aside a half hour to practice intentional time with God. It will not always produce a
burning bush, but the practice alone will allow for rest,
restoration, and a deeper intimacy with God. Write your
findings, thoughts, and impressions down, even if the
results are not what you were hoping for. As best you
can, make solitude part of your daily routine.

7

POKING HOLES IN THE DARKNESS

*You just stay here in this one corner of the Forest waiting for the
others to come to you. Why don't you go to them sometimes?*

A.A. Milne, *The House at Pooh Corner*[1]

When I was admitted to a psychiatric hospital for severe
depression at the age of 17, it was one of the most awful yet
significant times of my life. "Awful" and "significant" seem to like
one another. They make a show of acting like they have nothing in
common, but they are seen time and time again at the same parties.
They bump into one another so often I no longer think it's a coinci-
dence. I think awful and significant are in cahoots. They are book-
ends, each with their own shape but arriving as a set, holding up and
giving structure to all that stands between them.

I spent my first *awfulsignificant* night in that small padded room
alone, frightened, and humiliated. The next morning I met everyone else on the unit. They were equally terrifying. At that time, teen
psychiatric units were repositories for all the loose ends that parents, teachers, and society couldn't tie up properly. We each had
our own set of problems that prevented us from blending in with

others. Collectively, we were an odd bunch. Sure, we were all caught drawing outside the lines, but not one of us used the same color or instrument to do it. From drug addicts to schizophrenics, alcoholics to depressives, we were a robust and varied group, each in our own uniquely unsettling way.

Sam had a nose ring and blue Doc Martens boots that weighed at least eight pounds each. Sam was large and had language more colorful than tie-dyed pants. I never knew that one simple curse word could be used as an adjective, noun, conjunction, *and* verb in one sentence. Sam was a profanity poet. Sam was also a girl. Back then, her nose ring was alarmingly unusual. I didn't know anyone who had one. People with nose rings weren't part of everyday life like they are now. They didn't bag your groceries or fix your computer or teach at universities. They were on the outer fringe of society, smoking cigarettes and leaning against alley walls. I'm pretty sure nose rings would have been a uniform violation at my high school. We received a detention if our plaid skirts were more than two inches above the knee.

Nevertheless, there I was, in the same place as Sam. Her piercings nicely complemented her green hair, spiked dog collar, and T-shirt held together by safety pins. In all, Sam radiated angry rebellion. She was instantly annoyed by my very presence. There she stood, feet planted firmly on the ground, looking at me like I was a smudge.

Jenny had dyed orange hair and a sweet smile that showed off grayed gums and teeth. She was pale and slight. Despite the acne that interrupted her porcelain skin and the needle marks that peppered both arms, I thought she was beautiful. She had dark circles under her eyes that never quite disappeared, even when she wore makeup. She looked haunted and worn. She was gentle and skittish, like a sparrow.

Nick had long hair and loved heavy metal music. He wore a concert T-shirt every single day. The kind with black three-quarter-length sleeves and drawings on the front of bulging-eyed skeletons playing the drums. He was admitted because he was arrested for dealing marijuana. The judge said it was our hospital or juvenile hall. Nick chose us.

Michael was from Compton. I was told his mother admitted him because she didn't know what else to do. She was afraid for his future. He'd gotten mixed up with a gang called the Crips that was just emerging out of South Central Los Angeles. He wore a blue bandana somewhere on his body every day. Sometimes he was so out of control with rage that the staff would give him a Thorazine shot and put him in one of the solitary rooms until he calmed down. Michael never had much to do with me. I think I bored him, what with my wide-eyed naivety and constant crying.

There were about a dozen patients in all. We all had wildly different backgrounds and reasons for being there. Some kids had been there for months. Others were newbies like me. None of us claimed to like it. But secretly, in a place we would never admit out loud, I think every one of us knew we needed it.

It didn't take long to learn the routine. We were roused at the same time every day, given exactly enough time to take a shower and get dressed, and marched to the eating area as a group. During weekdays we had school. We sat together at the same large table in one room but worked independently. We continued to study the subjects we'd been learning before we arrived. There was a teacher there to supervise, but none of us accomplished much. In a normal high school setting, algebra feels irrelevant. It was downright comical in a place where we had all taken a Rorschach test an hour earlier.

In the afternoon we did art therapy. We drew pictures, painted, and created small projects that didn't involve scissors. I remember

Nick in his Metallica T-shirt as he crocheted a potholder and hummed Led Zeppelin songs. The evenings were spent in various forms of individual and group therapy. We sat in a circle and shared our feelings. It was just like the movie *One Flew Over the Cuckoo's Nest*, except our counselor (Brian) was way nicer than Nurse Ratched.

I told you earlier that I cried out to God the night I was admitted to the hospital. I said that God didn't answer. I told you I was sure He didn't give a fig about me. I knew I was a disappointment and a failure. I would never be invited into His exclusive club for people who had nice, neat feelings and who didn't drag thumbtacks across their arms. I told you that I didn't see God when I was in that psychiatric hospital.

But one of the graces of time is that it offers remembrance, and with remembrance comes perspective. It reveals what blessings were present yet undetected—like youth or love or innocence. It's only when you look back that you realize God was providing even when I didn't know it. I cried out for God. I wanted Him to show me He was there. In response, He sent me a bunch of teenagers who were nothing like me and who, I'm pretty sure, wanted to beat me up. They were just what I needed.

We're in This Together

> If the LORD had not been on our side—
>   let Israel say—
> if the LORD had not been on our side
>   when people attacked us,
> they would have swallowed us alive
>   when their anger flared against us;
> the flood would have engulfed us,
>   the torrent would have swept over us,

> the raging waters
>> would have swept us away.
> Praise be to the LORD,
>> who has not let us be torn by their teeth.
> We have escaped like a bird
>> from the fowler's snare;
> the snare has been broken,
>> and we have escaped.
> Our help is in the name of the LORD,
>> the Maker of heaven and earth (Psalm 124:1-8).

The majority of David's psalms are written from a first-person perspective: "*I* thirst for you, *my* whole being longs for you" (Psalm 63:1, emphasis added). His psalms are so personal in nature that it's like eavesdropping on private conversations with God. But Psalm 124 is different. There is not one "I" statement in it. This is a communal prayer. This isn't just David talking; this is all of God's people reflecting on their journey thus far. Many people. One song.

This psalm is like that moment at a rock concert when the lead singer stops singing and lets the crowd take over. The entire audience sings in unison, knowing the lyrics so well they belt them out on cue. They are no longer spectators. They are part of the music. They *are* the music. They've listened to and sung this song in the privacy of their home, car, and shower. But now, crowded in with thousands of others, what was once a personal experience has become a corporate one. They are together, sharing the passion for music in concert with each other. Voices are lifted high and strong, confident and unified. It's a sacred, shared moment.

David wrote the soundtrack to Midnight and we're all invited to join in. Every person walking this planet has a story of hardship and grief. Each one of us can attest to the torrent that threatened to sweep over us. And because we are followers of Jesus Christ, each one of us can tell stories of His faithfulness.

Midnight is a time when you might question more, doubt more, fear more. That's okay. It's part of the journey. But to forget God's faithfulness is to forgo half the story. The torrents are real, but so is the Lord who will not let us be torn by them. This psalm declares God's faithfulness. It is your song too. It is a declaration of hope born in hopeless surroundings.

Eugene Peterson says, "Psalm 124 is an instance of a person who digs deeply into the trouble and finds there the presence of God who is on our side. In the details of a conflict, in the minuteness of a personal history, the majestic greatness of God becomes revealed. Faith develops out of the most difficult aspects of our existence, not the easiest."[2] To sing in the darkness is to declare that the sacred is still present. It is to embolden our hearts with the truth of the mighty God who goes before us, behind us, and beside us. He is swirling in the midst of our deepest anguish and encircling us with people who ensure we are not alone. God is faithful. He will rescue you from this pain. He will save you from anything that threatens to take you away from Him. Declare what you have seen Him do. Assert what you see Him doing now. If you are experiencing present defeat, sing of past victories.

At church on Sundays, I love to stand next to someone who really knows how to carry a tune. It makes me feel like I have a better voice than I actually do. Their ability to hit the right notes smooths over my inability to do anything else than make a joyful noise. I like to lean in close to them. I ride on their coattails of blessing.

Community offers you the chance to worship in unison with others. Even when your throat is dry and you forget the words, you are surrounded by those who can sing for you. When you hear others' stories of God's faithfulness, they can bolster your own faith. You can ride on their coattails of blessing. You are beloved by the same God as those with stories of hope and redemption. You are walking out your faith on a road that has been traveled before. You are not alone. You are part of a chorus.

It's Necessary

From time to time, you will be convinced that it's safest for all involved if you keep to yourself. Maybe you're afraid you'll hurt someone with words you don't mean. Maybe you're terrified you will be misunderstood by those you love. Maybe you're afraid that if you tell the people you need most about the depth of your sadness, you will scare them off completely. Midnight is so vulnerable and your struggles are so personal that it feels risky to reach out to others. If you do, you might be disappointed by the response.

Those who are closest to you are the ones most impacted by your Midnight. They will see your pain and will want to help you. You will want them to help you. But your attempts to describe what is happening and their attempts to see you through this time could cause deep frustration on both sides. The more they try to help, the more it will become clear that your friends and family do not understand all you are experiencing. It will make you feel more alone than before. You might decide it's best to roam the earth alone, like in those television shows where the main character wanders from town to town to meet friendly strangers, teach a valuable lesson, then move on before anyone gets too attached.

Avoiding unnecessary hurt is reasonable. We have enough agony in this world without inviting it over for a cup of tea. However, some pain is necessary. Like physical therapy after surgery or endurance training before a marathon, necessary pain moves us toward strength and healing. It might kick our behind in the process, but it develops and defines the places that have been lacking. Community is one of those providers of necessary pain, because it is a provider of necessary healing.

There will be times in this Midnight when people will drive you crazy. When friends call, it's annoying. If they don't, it's hurtful. Your spouse will say all the wrong things at exactly the wrong time. The more wounded you are, the more you will experience a steady stream of offense, misunderstanding, and unreasonableness from everyone within a 50-mile radius. You will become increasingly impatient. You will be tempted to kick the dog. Your friends, your family, the lady in front of you in line at the grocery store will all seem to be conspiring against you, working in subtle yet intentional ways to push you right over the edge.

Some days it is hard to get out of bed. Can't we just sleep our way through all of this? Nope. Even if you are incredibly wealthy, have Mary Poppins to care for your kids and a swarm of servants to do your errands, it is not a good idea to retire from the world for long periods of time. Especially when you are deeply struggling. Solitude is vital and rest is restorative, but if you've been in your pajamas for more than four days and are not running a fever, it's time for community.

Staying away from the world when you are in pain will not alleviate your problems. It might help maintain your dignity, but it will not heal your wounds. You end up in a bad neighborhood when you try to navigate heartbreak on your own. You are not created or equipped to do that. At the creation of Adam, God said, "It is not good for the man to be alone" (Genesis 2:18). The same is true for you.

God has fashioned us to need one another. It's in our very DNA. Even the Lone Ranger had Tonto. To think you will somehow be able to navigate this dark night of the soul on your own is just not possible. That's why you have community.

In this Midnight there are obligations you'll need to release. But if you have participated at all in your first few decades here on the planet, there will be demands you still need to meet. Errands to run, calls to make, jobs to do, pets and family to attend to. Your boss will not stop expecting you to do your job because you are in Midnight. Bosses are funny that way; they expect you to work for your paycheck. If you have kids, well, forget about taking six months off to go find yourself. They need help with their homework.

All these demands are going to feel loud and harsh. They might overwhelm you. You will feel resentful that so much is being asked of you when you have so little to give. But the mundane tasks of your life are vital. The needs of others are essential to your own. They make you get out of bed and get dressed. Paying bills and dropping off the dry cleaning serve as reminders that Midnight cannot rob you of everything. They force you to recall your life before all of this happened. When you continue to do what is necessary, they guarantee you will have a life to come back to when the sun rises.

Midnight work is different than daylight work, but it's still work. Because this time of darkness is fashioned for more than heartache, it will require some effort. Part of that effort needs to go toward reaching out to others. Even if you cannot fully explain it, confess what is happening to you. Let a few trusted people into this journey. Be kind to them. Be patient. Even if it seems like they are trying to drive you to the brink of madness, it's rarely true. Most likely, they want to help even if they are clumsy about it. Let them in. Midnight is too vast to travel alone.

Smoky Grace

I gave my life to Christ in my mid-twenties. It radically changed everything. It was like going from living in shades of gray to a full prism of color. Everything was vivid and beautiful. For my first three years of Christianity, I experienced more joy than I ever thought possible. But as I discussed in the introduction, depression wormed its way back into my life. I was utterly confused. I had a great marriage, two great kids, I loved my church, and I loved my friends. Even so, the darkness descended once more. I was devastated.

When I finally decided to meet with a Christian counselor, he suggested I go on medication for a while. Until that point, I had only used medication during those awful couple of years surrounding my hospitalization. After so much time and so many changes since then, it was devastating to consider medication once again. I didn't know what to do.

I was attending a Bible study group at the time, so I decided to share with the leader what I was facing. I stayed behind after the group left and poured out my heart to her. I relayed my fear of going on medication. I shared my devastation over struggling with depression again. She listened well and prayed with me. I left feeling a bit lighter.

The following day, the pastor of our church called me. My Bible study leader had told him everything I'd shared with her in confidence. Apparently, she no longer wanted me in the Bible study. She thought that because I didn't act depressed or talk about it with the group, I was being deceitful. (Some people don't realize that you can have depression and still function.) I was devastated and humiliated. The pastor brought us together in an attempt to help us work things out, but the damage was done. If Billy Graham himself were in that study, I wouldn't have gone back.

I'm sure it will not shock you to know that, after that, I was afraid to tell anyone about my medication dilemma. But eventually I needed to talk about it. I decided to trust my friend Michelle with my secret. Michelle is the least churchy Christian I know. At the time, she had spiky pink hair. She smoked like a chimney. She didn't read the Bible a lot. Her overall theology was summed up as, "I don't know much, but I know I love Jesus."

Michelle and I tried to exercise together every so often. I think we were hoping 45-minute walks once a week would produce six-pack abs. Between my french fry habit and her lighting a cigarette every 20 minutes, we never came close. Nonetheless, being the dedicated hardbodies we pretended to be, we pressed on.

It was on one of those walks that the dam finally burst. I told Michelle everything. I cried and talked and cried some more. I told her about my history of depression and my hospitalization. I told her how I was back in counseling and about the medication. I was sure I was failing Christianity 101. I blubbered on for about 30 minutes until I ran out of words and tears. Then Michelle cleared her throat, took a long drag of her cigarette, and said, "Dude, if the medication helps you, then who cares?" And that was it. After all my ranting and raving, all my words, all those tears, one simple sentence was the sum total of Michelle's advice. It was exactly what I needed.

Michelle took the massive issue that was overwhelming me and shrunk it down to something manageable. She saw all my crazy and wasn't intimidated by it or swallowed up by it. She didn't judge. She didn't shame. She showed me more about Jesus in one sentence than the Bible study leader ever did in all my weeks with her. Not only did Michelle share my burden, she reduced it to a controllable weight. It was now one I could bear, because she was now carrying it with me. In a plume of tobacco smoke, Michelle demonstrated how the grace of God works within the community of His people. I will forever be grateful to her.

If you, like me, lean toward morbid introspection, it's your friends who will pull your head out of your nether regions. When you get moody and morose and start writing bad poetry, they can remind you that you are by no means the worst person in the world. Of course, if they know you well, they are equally able to remind you that you aren't Mother Teresa either. You desperately need both of these reality checks.

The people in your life will rescue you from the bad neighborhood of self-pity. They will help steer you back to bigger, less myopic spaces and smaller, more manageable problems. They are the antidote to self-centeredness. Do not push away people who love you. Pick up the phone when they call. Answer their texts. And for Pete's sake, get dressed and go on a walk with them once in a while.

Midnight is a journey of the soul. It is carving out new places inside of you. Like anything worthwhile, it's going to take some time. Going to dinner with friends will not stop the process. If anything, it will allow Midnight to continue to do its work. Making a point to be with others will remind you what daylight feels like even if you aren't there yourself.

Glimmers of light in dark places don't just happen between you and God, they appear in the form of people. You are surrounded in your Midnight by small, shining stars that point to goodness and light. They will not remove your pain in one moment, but they will serve as proof that light is still peeking through the dark places.

Your friends, your spouse, your kids who still want dinner no matter how awful you feel will keep you tethered to a world bigger than your own heartache. They are living, breathing reminders that it is not all about you. And if life isn't all about you, that means your depression, anxiety, sickness, or anything else you've got going doesn't have the power to rob you of everything. It is not bigger than God. It is limited. There are too many stars for the sky to ever go pitch black. The people in your life don't need to understand your Midnight in order to be part of it. Let them in. Prepare to be misunderstood from time to time. Let them in anyway. It will be hard. You will feel vulnerable. And they will help heal your heart.

The Church

It's cumbersome and weird to explain to your church community what is happening when you are in the midst of Midnight. One doesn't just walk up to people and say, "Hey, I'm in the throes of some superbad anxiety and depression. Want to hang out?" Awkward. Hopefully, you have entrusted a few close people with the particulars of your story. But sometimes you'll run into those who have no idea how to respond, so they choose no response at all.

This dynamic plays out in churches all the time. For instance, a couple is going through a really, really hard time. Their marriage ends in divorce. It gets really bumbling from there, because no one quite knows what to do. Along with the kids, the house, and the dishes, the couple has to decide who gets the church. After all, they both can't be attending on Sunday; that's just too odd for everyone involved. What do you chat about at the coffee kiosk between services? Asking questions about the divorce is fraught with relational, theological, and personal land mines, and yet *not* asking about it feels like ignoring the elephant in the middle of the sanctuary.

Many times, people in the midst of Midnight don't receive the care they need, not because they are uncared for, but because people in the congregation simply don't know what to say. In the case of a divorce, the couple isn't sure what to do or say either. So no one does or says anything. Eventually, each ex-spouse leaves the church because it's all so painful and awkward. After a year or so, both find their own new church. Some in the congregation might know vaguely about their past difficulties, but that was in the past. The wound isn't oozing blood all over the foyer carpet. It's tidier. It's much easier on everyone if the worst parts of grief, divorce, depression, or other forms of Midnight are not happening in real time. That way, everyone can acknowledge it without feeling completely helpless. It's like those documentaries about famous movie stars who went through horrible times. Sure, they were an alcoholic and their lives were circling the drain, but that was ten years ago and look how wonderfully they are doing now! It's much easier if our downfalls are neatly stored in the past. No one wants their own brand of crazy bursting through the church doors on a Sunday morning, displaying its wares without a tidy ending in sight.

I'm sure you can see the problem with this tendency. First, it's not good for anyone involved. Each spouse is left to navigate heartbreak on their own. Losing their church community just adds to their isolation. It's also a terrible formula for the church body. If we just hold our breath and wait until the most uncomfortable people in our church go somewhere else, we're not learning to practice deep, abiding agape love. Furthermore, it teaches us that when it's our Midnight, we cannot rely on the church to see us through it. But there is another way.

What if churches embraced those in the midst of Midnight? What if the dark night of the soul is talked about from the pulpit, in groups, and at the coffee kiosk? What if the pain of divorce, depression, grief, and struggle is woven into the fabric of the conversations we have with one another? Every person on this planet will face the unthinkable. We will all be confronted at one point or another with pain that leaves us helpless and stumbling in the dark. For some, it will come in the form of illness. In others, it will be the destruction of a marriage. Unexpected circumstances will occur in the most unexpected families. We all end up in places we never wanted to be. We might as well be in them together.

The church is the place where we should be able to find our first, best, and last hope. It is the place where we should be able to go with our deepest pain and hardest questions about life, God, and the meaning of terrible circumstances. That kind of pain doesn't look good on the brochure, but if we leave it off, we are not telling the truth about the Christian journey, let alone the human journey. We're not telling the truth about ourselves. And we are not telling the truth about God. If Midnight is part of the rhythm God allows, and if it truly offers more than darkness, then it needs to be talked about again and again in both the large and small aspects of church life.

This will take practice on everyone's part. Let's face it: If we try to stay present with one another in the awful places, it's going to be weird for everyone. The temptation to avoid the whole mess will be strong and steady. But if we do not hang in there with one another, if we cannot bear one another's burdens, then we will not be able to bear our own. We will live in isolation, apart from the community God has given us. We will miss out on one of His richest gifts.

Rick Warren is the founder of Saddleback Church in Lake Forest, California. It is one of the largest churches in the United States. Rick is known around the world for his vision, faith, and writing, including his bestselling book *The Purpose Driven Life*. But even amazing church leaders are not exempt from Midnight, and neither are their children. On April 5, 2013, Rick and Kay Warren's son Matthew committed suicide. He battled mental illness his entire life. The news of his death brought international attention, along with the speculation, conversation, and accusations any piece of sensational news brings. It was an especially hot topic because the Warrens are Christians.

The reputation of the Christian church to those outside it is dicey. A lot of people accuse us of hypocrisy. They think we are stuck up, judgmental, and self-righteous. A lot of the time they are correct. The church is made up of terribly flawed people, some of whom do and say unimaginably cruel things in the name of Jesus. Many times the church is the army that shoots their own soldiers, especially when they're already wounded. It's agonizing and disappointing.

And yet, despite all the church's failings, there is nothing like it. Established by Jesus Christ, ordained by His sacrifice and eternal love, it is a demonstration of God's passion for every living soul. The church is capable of stepping in where others run. The church can bless, feed, comfort, and build. It is responsible for great works of compassion and small acts of kindness. The church has been an influential part of history since its inception. It has served as a sanctuary and a sentry. The church stands so that no one has to go through Midnight by themselves. It can penetrate the darkest places with the light of Christ. It is capable of enormous good.

Almost a year after Matthew's death, Saddleback Church formed the Conference on the Church and Mental Health. It "amassed 3,000 registrants and features a lineup of pastors, academics and psychiatrists hosting panels and prayers to tackle the stigma of mental illness and suicide in the church."[3] The meeting was broadcast online and was available worldwide. The church that made its mark on the world through creativity and savvy evangelism wove the issues of mental illness into the fabric of their culture. They started Hope for Mental Health, a resource for those struggling with mental illness and the people who love them. Their website states, "Studies show that when people are struggling with mental illness, the first place they call is the church. Let's be ready."[4] Saddleback Church boldly walked into the pitch of Midnight to seek out those who are lost in it.

If their son's suicide made Rick and Kay Warren want to slip into obscurity, I wouldn't have blamed them a bit. Their grief was on display for the world to see, and their personal tragedy became a national curiosity. All kinds of people, Christians and unbelievers alike, drummed up theories and accusations about the Warrens' parenting, faith, and church. Reporters picked through their lives, behaving as though they were not real people who had just experienced a profound tragedy. At its worst, the news media reduced Matthew and his parents to a sound bite.

But even in the chaos, the Warrens refused to keep their Midnight tightly to themselves. They asked for help. Warren sent a letter to his congregation saying, "I've been your pastor for 33 years, I need you now, I need you to pastor me for this time."[5] Their vulnerability in the face of deep tragedy was generous and profound. Rick and Kay shared their personal grief, and in doing so they brought mental illness out of the shadows. They not only spent the time they needed to in their Midnight, but they created a venue where others can be sought out in the midst of theirs.

Church is a complicated place. No one inside or outside of it likes to deal with messy, painful, uncomfortable things. Whether it's mental health, grief, divorce, or death, the big topics will make our hearts dip and our stomachs churn. We will want to solve things quickly and easily. It is not possible. We will be tempted to abandon painful topics altogether. It's not acceptable.

Jesus Christ got really messy. He taught the working class and the wealthy. He dined with Pharisees and prostitutes. He touched the diseased, the outcasts, the demon-possessed, and the lepers. There was never a mess He wasn't willing to walk into. He gave His life in a horrifying, messy way so we never have to be alone in ours. If He did that, then His church can stand with people in their mess as well. With broken hearts and brave faith, Rick and Kay Warren have led the way.

If you are part of a church, bring your Midnight with you through the doors. Talk about what is happening. You don't need to attend Sunday services with puffy eyes and snot running from your nose, although if the alternative is staying home, then go for it. You don't need to tell everyone what is going on with you. Your journey is intensely personal, and it may not even be appropriate. But you need to tell *someone* in the church. Preferably more than one person. If your church offers support groups, attend. If they don't have anything, ask. If they do nothing, find a church that will.

Like your friends, various churches will respond differently. Find safe people who will stick with you. They don't need to be perfect, just safe enough. Even if they don't handle things exactly how you'd wish, if they respond with compassion and empathy, they are probably safe enough.

We all need safe-enough churches that will support us. Both our community of people and the church will absolutely, positively disappoint us from time to time. Both will leave us yearning for something more, something better, something strong enough to enter into all of this with you. But they are not supposed to be able to handle it entirely. We can forgive them for not meeting all our needs. We can withstand it when we are misunderstood. We can find tremendous comfort even if they cannot offer it as often or as intuitively as we'd hoped. We need them. Better yet, they are not our only source of support. We have God Himself.

The Gift of Community

> She saw the streak as a vast swinging bridge extending upward from the earth through a field of living fire. Upon it a vast horde of souls were rumbling toward heaven. There were whole companies of white-trash, cleaned for the first time in their lives…and battalions of freaks and lunatics shouting and clapping and leaping like frogs…In the woods around her the invisible cricket choruses had struck up, but what she heard were the voices of the souls climbing upward into the starry field and shouting hallelujah.
>
> —FLANNERY O'CONNOR, *REVELATION*[6]

It didn't take more than two days for me to discover that I loved my scary, strange roommates at the psychiatric hospital. Sure, we all had vastly different backgrounds, problems, and tastes in fashion. But once I figured out I wasn't going to die or get shanked, I discovered how much in common I had with Sam, Jenny, Michael, Nick, and the others.

Every one of us at that hospital were the walking wounded. We were grasping for anything that brought relief from the terror, the anger, the hopelessness we felt inside. Some of us grasped for that relief by getting high. Some of us did it by cutting ourselves. Some of us tried to bury it so deep that it was killing us from the inside out. It didn't matter that our paths would have never crossed on the outside. We were soldered together in the crucible of heartbreak. The commonality of pain opened our eyes. We *saw* one another. It was there, in that *awfulsignificant* setting of a psychiatric hospital that I discovered I was not alone in the darkness.

Until I was forced to be part of a community, I was convinced the darkness would destroy me. I didn't know how to express the torrent of emotions that swirled around inside. I was sure I was too odd, too strange, too much, and not enough to be understood or loved by anyone. That *awfulsignificant* experience of being forced into a psychiatric hospital gave me my voice. By hearing the stories of others, I discovered my own. Conversely, when I finally started to talk about my depression, it allowed others to talk about theirs. Together, we formed a chorus.

I cried out to God to come to me in that hospital and He did. He showed up with a nose ring. He used salty language. His arms were peppered with needle marks. He listened to Metallica. God made Himself known by the people I met there. By granting me friends who understood my heartache, He showed me a glimpse of Himself. He ushered me into the community of the brokenhearted; it's

His community too. In the loneliest time of my life, the God who I was sure abandoned me didn't leave me alone for a minute. He surrounded me with people. He surrounded me with Himself.

Depression, pain, and grief will try to convince you that Midnight is a place of desolation. With all your strange feelings and weird thoughts and crazy insecurities, pain will say there is no room for you in community. It's a lie.

This whole world is made up of misfits. Every one of us have parts that are mangled and marred. Jesus Christ died on the cross and rose from the grave because He would not let brokenness have the last word. In the greatest *awfulsignificant* act of love ever known, He defeated desolation. He ensured that Midnight would never be a solitary place. It is dark but it is not without light. You are not alone. Look up. Look around. Find the small stars surrounding you, poking holes through the darkness.

The gift of community is that it's living, breathing, physical proof you are not alone. Every person walking the planet has their own story of fierceness and longing. You will only find them if you seek them out. You will discover your commonalities with the most unexpected people. Some might have green hair or smoke like a chimney. You will discover the other misfits of this world when you listen for their voices. They will help you find yours in return.

You are part of us: the community of the brokenhearted. You belong here. We need you here. There is room for you at this table of suffering and joy, faith and terror. You belong here because you were made to experience community with yourself, God, and others.

One day, we will be in a place where we will see with unclouded vision. Our voices will be a chorus of never-ending praise to the God who has made us whole. Until then, we will sing in the dark places. We will declare God's faithfulness in the center of our trouble.

We will tell our stories of torrents and raging waters and snares because we have a God who has rescued us before and *will* rescue us again from all of it. We are the community of the brokenhearted who will sing of the God who has not let us be torn. Our help is in the name of the Lord, the Maker of heaven and earth. And all God's people said, "Amen."

MOONLIGHT MEDITATIONS

- How has God showed up in unexpected ways in this Midnight?
- What do you need from your church? How might you participate in getting those needs met?
- Who are the people in your life that point you to God's faithfulness?
- When has God been faithful to see you through waters that threatened to drown you? Use those times to strengthen you in your current situation.

EVENING STROLL

- Send a card, note, or email to someone who inspires you. Tell them how they have influenced you with the way they live. Then send one to a person who needs encouragement. Remind them they are not alone.
- Resolve to get connected and stay connected to at least a few people. Moreover, take the initiative to find a community who can journey with you. It might take the form of group therapy, a church, or even a book club or

scrapbooking group. They just need to be people who
are honest, real, and looking for community too. Even
when it is hard or uncomfortable, make the effort to
meet with them regularly. Allow community to become
a habit.

8

FEAR NOT

Fear is the emotion that makes us blind.

STEPHEN KING[1]

I've always believed in God. I've never seriously questioned His existence. But what I believe about God has changed dramatically. Early in my battle with depression, I was sure God was bitterly disappointed in me. I didn't think He liked me very much. Or even that He knew me very well. When scanning the expanse of His creation, I believed His eyes would land on me for a millisecond and move on, uninterested in what He saw. I imagined He didn't have much use for the redheaded girl crying in the corner.

Later, when I placed my faith in Jesus Christ, I was sure He would immediately send me to work in a third-world country. I was convinced my first test of faith would be to live as a missionary in a place where they didn't have toilet paper. I assumed He was going to make me do things I didn't want to do to prove my loyalty. Trust was clearly an issue.

People have been making up stories about God for a long time. Some people imagine Him to be the giant Santa Claus in the sky, bestowing gifts to the kids who behave. Others think He is a sadist, gleefully inflicting pain without rhyme or reason. Still others believe He got the ball rolling with creation and then left us alone to manage it.

What do you believe about God? I'm not asking what you think you should say about God. I'm not asking for the "correct" answer. You might know the Bible backward and forward. That has little to do with my question. What do you actually, in the depths of your soul, believe about God? If you are not sure how you would answer that question, fear is a great way to find out.

Don't You Care?

> That day when evening came, [Jesus] said to his disciples, "Let us go over to the other side." Leaving the crowd behind, they took him along, just as he was, in the boat. There were also other boats with him. A furious squall came up, and the waves broke over the boat, so that it was nearly swamped. Jesus was in the stern, sleeping on a cushion. The disciples woke him and said to him, "Teacher, don't you care if we drown?"
>
> He got up, rebuked the wind and said to the waves, "Quiet! Be still!" Then the wind died down and it was completely calm.
>
> He said to his disciples, "Why are you so afraid? Do you still have no faith?"
>
> They were terrified and asked each other, "Who is this? Even the wind and the waves obey him!" (Mark 4:35-41).

At this point in the Gospel of Mark, the disciples have been with Jesus for some time. Thus far, they've left their nets and decided to follow Him (Mark 1:18). They have seen Him heal a man who was demon possessed (Mark 1:25), Peter's mother-in-law (Mark 1:31), crowds of people with various ailments (Mark 1:34), a person with leprosy (Mark 1:44), a person who was paralyzed (Mark 2:12), and a man with a withered hand (Mark 3:5). Additionally, He has been teaching the crowds with the authority of God (Mark 1:27). So one would think they'd feel safe around Jesus. Like He's in control. Like He's got their back. Yeah, not so much.

In Mark 4:35, Jesus invited His disciples to get into their boats. They quickly found themselves in all sorts of trouble. In the middle of the night, a huge storm erupted. Waves crashed. Wind howled. Water poured in. And where was Jesus? Asleep. Yes, that's what the Scripture says. It was an all-hands-on-deck emergency and Jesus was asleep in the middle of it all.

Oh my, oh my. This is so affirming. If you have ever wondered if Jesus is asleep in the middle of your crisis, here is your answer. He might be. But how you interpret His inactivity reveals what you believe about Him.

The disciples took one look at Jesus and assumed the worst. They thought His nap meant He didn't care. Their fear revealed their doubts about God. Sure, He could heal people and feed thousands and cast out demons. But deep down in their souls, His closest followers did not entirely trust Him.

The storm had the potential to drown the disciples. It was truly a life-threatening situation. The waves and wind were real. But Jesus was there too. He was real too. And He wasn't worried. He was the one who invited them to get into the boat in the first place. He actually invited them into the storm. It was a fearful situation, but they had nothing to fear.

As Stephen King wrote, fear blinds. It will confuse your thoughts. It will make you assume things about God and yourself that are simply untrue. Fear will try to drown you in hopelessness and panic. Its insidious nature slips inside your heart throughout your life. Fear is learned. It is fed and watered by all we cannot control. It doesn't just arrive when things get scary. Fear finds its way into the heart long before the sun sets and Midnight approaches.

The disciples' terror revealed the doubts that already lurked inside them. The storm only confirmed the fears they already had. Was Jesus truly God? Did He really love them? Was He the Savior? The questions they could ignore in the calm arose in the whipping wind. They were in dangerous waters, but it was fear that made them believe things about Jesus that just weren't true.

At Midnight, your fears will rise up from your stomach and spread into every cell of your body. They will make their way into your throat and try to choke you into submission. They will take this opportunity to prove you have a reason to be afraid. You will be tempted to let the fearful aspects of Midnight confirm all your worst doubts about God.

I've lived with panic attacks for as long as I can remember. They hurl toward me at the speed of sound. When a panic attack hits, it takes over my whole body. Sometimes it is so acute I feel paralyzed. It is difficult to think or speak when the anxiety is severe. It feels like all my circuits go on overload. Every fiber of my being is afraid. Sometimes I know what caused the panic. Sometimes I don't. When I am that overwhelmed, it doesn't really matter. All I know is I feel like I might die of fear.

One of the best things about experiencing such deep anxiety for so long is that it's given me a lot of practice. Like Jane Goodall living with the chimpanzees in Africa, I have studied my fear in its natural habitat. I've learned its habits. I've become an expert on my fear. It hasn't made the panic attacks disappear, but at least I know what to expect when they arrive.

The most significant thing I have learned about panic attacks is they do not last. For years, those panic attacks tried to convince me they would. They'd tell me I had no power over them, I was helpless in the storm, and I would drown in my anxiety. But then something changed. Just one thought was enough to dramatically shift my experience of panic attacks.

One day, in the middle of anxiety profound enough to send me crawling under the covers, a tiny thought emerged. I had the sense that Jesus was sitting on the edge of the bed with me. He was right there, patiently waiting with me for the storm to pass. Jesus wasn't afraid of my fear. He was looking at me with acceptance and warmth. Jesus was as real as my panic. He wasn't overwhelmed by how overwhelmed I felt. This tiny realization shifted something inside of me. If Jesus wasn't dismayed by my fear, perhaps I didn't need to be either. Maybe it was enough to ride it out, knowing it would end and knowing He was with me.

As much as fear is part of every Midnight, so is Jesus. He is woven into your experience, bringing His radiance into the darkness. Anxiety is temporary. Jesus is permanent. Your Savior is not overwhelmed by what overwhelms you. This truth may not cradicate fear altogether, but it will put fear in its place.

Fear blinded the disciples from seeing what was right in front of them. Jesus was with them in the middle of the storm. He never left. The storm wasn't too much for Him. As a matter of fact, the storm was so insignificant to Jesus that He was sleeping right through it. Even though they assumed the worst about Him, the disciples eventually turned to Jesus. It was their one redeeming action. They panicked, they cried, and they were overtaken by fear. Nonetheless, they called out to their Savior, and Jesus answered.

Observe that Jesus was stirred to action not by their amazing faith but by their cries of fear. He was roused by their weakness. It wasn't thunder or lightning or cold water sloshing into the boat that woke Him up. Those didn't matter. Jesus reacted only when He heard the desperate need of the people He loved.

Rather than try to rid yourself of fear, invite Jesus into it. See the waters rise and pour in, feel the wild winds of your emotion, experience the tossing and turning in your soul. Allow the fear to come. When it does, call out to Jesus. Tell Him how afraid you are. Tell Him about the waves and winds. Ask Him to find you in the middle of this downpour. Your candid cries matter to Jesus; they awaken and move Him. In turn, your soul will be awakened to Him who has been with you in the storm all along.

You have a God who is gracious enough to respond not only to your faith but to your lack of it. Fear will cloud your vision and weaken your resolve, but it cannot keep you from the love of Christ. Confessing your fear and crying out to God in the midst of it is the first step toward courage.

God Doesn't Use Red Pen

In both the Old and New Testaments, God tells His people, "Fear not." This immediately makes me feel like a failure. If I could "fear not" at will, I'd have half the wrinkles and twice the laugh lines. Instead, I have two deep furrows between my eyebrows. I want to fear not, but I'm not very good at it. I'm too afraid.

It is completely understandable if you are feeling more than a little terrified in this Midnight. The dark restricts your ability to see more than the next step, so your pace might have slowed to a hesitant shuffle. The solitary nature of your experience can eat away your confidence. This is a time when you are vulnerable and have little ability to defend yourself against the onslaught of emotion. It's no wonder if you feel a bit panicked.

Fear doesn't mean you are bombing Christianity. You are not failing at faith and you are not blowing it with Jesus. This is not a test of faith with a pass-fail grade. Sometimes I hear people in hard times say something like, "God is testing me," and I cringe a little. God does indeed test us, but when I hear someone talking about God testing them, most of the time the implication is that they need to get it right. The idea is that God has passed out a number-two pencil and college-ruled paper and you better know the answers or you will get a big, fat *F* on your paper. But this Midnight is not like your eleventh-grade history final. This is not a grading situation. God doesn't use red pen. And He isn't disappointed with you because you are afraid.

In *The Gift of Fear*, Gavin de Becker wrote:

> Real fear is a signal intended to be a very brief, mere servant of intuition. But though few would argue that extended, unanswered fear is destructive, millions choose to stay there. They may have forgotten or never learned that fear is not an emotion like sadness or happiness, either of which might last a long while. It is not a state, like anxiety. True fear is a survival signal that sounds only in the presence of danger, yet unwarranted fear has assumed a power over us that it holds over no other creature on earth.[2]

Healthy fear is useful. It ensures you wear a seat belt and prevents you from cuddling with porcupines. Only deeply disturbed people lack all precaution. The problem most of the time is that the fear you live with is not the kind that is helpful to your survival. It is not protecting you from heartbreak or pain. If you have relied upon your fear to keep you safe, fear is not serving you well. It is assuming a power over you that is inappropriate and untenable. It is making your life small. It is weakening your stamina. And it is keeping you unbalanced.

James 1:2-4 says, "Consider it pure joy, my brothers and sisters, whenever you face trials of many kinds, because you know that the testing of your faith produces perseverance. Let perseverance finish its work so that you may be mature and complete, not lacking in anything." In Greek, the word "perseverance" in this verse means patience. It means faithful endurance.[3] And we only endure the things that are not easy. Difficult circumstances are what build faith and strength. The goal is not destruction. It is building up.

When you exercise your body, the only way to build muscle is to stress it. The only way to gain strength is to discover weakness, assess it, and challenge it. When your faith is tested, it is strained, but it is strengthened too. Time, repetition, and tremendous purpose give the payoff of a mature, developed faith.

Perhaps you've equated "fear not" to that age-old, sage advice to "calm down." Not helpful. Has anyone, in the history of human-kind, ever actually calmed down after hearing such a trite sugges-tion? Could any two words be more useless? The terrible advice to calm down assumes you have decided, with clarity and forethought, to make the decision to panic. I mean, who wants fear? No one. But you don't have to be fearless to fear not. As a matter of fact, courage and fear always go together. Courage only works within the confines of the terrifying. It's not courageous to do something that doesn't scare you. Walking into the shallow end of a swimming pool is noth-ing if you've been swimming your whole life, but it's everything for the person who is terrified of water. To trust God with your fear is part of the delicate, diligent work of strengthening your faith.

My friend Liz is the fiercest woman of faith I know. In 2001, she decided to start a school. Like, a *real* school with kids and parents and teachers and fire drills. She began with two borrowed church classrooms and 28 students. Since then, Trinity Classical Academy has grown into a thriving institution of over 500 students from kin-dergarten through twelfth grade. The kids learn Latin. They study the arts and church history. They honor God. They learn to debate, to think, to question, and to discover. They play all kinds of sports and have a boatload of fun too. Liz has changed a lot of lives with her vision, and more students come every year.

In leading and developing the school, she has navigated countless hurdles: budgets, real estate, difficult students, difficult parents, certifications, ordinances, and fund-raising. She seems to do it all with such confidence. Even the blessings of grateful families, generous donors, happy students, and dedicated teachers carry heavy responsibility. And yet she's out every morning, greeting the students as they enter. She remembers every child's name. She is always armed with Starbucks and her cell phone. She takes on more in one day than I do in a year. I marvel at her determination to make a difference in this world. I asked her if she's ever afraid. "Every day. Every single day," she said. "But I just do it afraid."

Courage never feels like it looks. Most courageous people wouldn't describe themselves as brave. They most likely don't feel courageous. They feel like Liz. Afraid. And then they do what they need to do anyway.

If you are waiting to feel courageous during this Midnight, you will probably be waiting for a long time. You cannot will yourself to be brave. You can't just close your eyes tight and try really hard.

When God says, "Fear not," He is not coming at you with some banal advice to calm down in a situation where you are overwhelmed. He is never condescending to His children. His yoke is easy and His burden is light (Matthew 11:30). He is not making impossible demands on you, so don't make them on yourself.

Fear not means there is nothing to actually be afraid of. God is present and in control. Fear isn't necessary. It will not protect you. It is not useful and you cannot trust what it is telling you. It will only confuse and distract you. Unfettered fear will make the ground shift beneath your feet. It will pull your focus away from everything that matters.

Even if fear is your first reaction to the unknown of Midnight, it doesn't need to be your only one. Despite what the adorable signs in Hobby Lobby say, it is almost impossible to "Be Fearless" in frightening circumstances. Fortunately, courage doesn't require fearlessness. You just need to know what to do when the fear comes.

Armor

Ephesians 6:10-17 is a rallying cry to Christians everywhere. The words are part of a letter that Paul wrote to the Ephesian church, but wouldn't it make a fantastic speech? I picture a handsome Hollywood star wearing leather, mounted on a horse, and speaking these words to masses of people while the wind blows his perfectly coiffed hair:

> Finally, be strong in the Lord and in his mighty power. Put on the full armor of God, so that you can take your stand against the devil's schemes. For our struggle is not against flesh and blood, but against the rulers, against the authorities, against the powers of this dark world and against the spiritual forces of evil in the heavenly realms. Therefore put on the full armor of God, so that when the day of evil comes, you may be able to stand your ground, and after you have done everything, to stand. Stand firm then, with the belt of truth buckled around your waist, with the breastplate of righteousness in place, and with your feet fitted with the readiness that comes from the gospel of peace. In addition to all this, take up the shield of faith, with which you can extinguish all the flaming arrows of the evil one. Take the helmet of salvation and the sword of the Spirit, which is the word of God (Ephesians 6:10-17).

These words stir the imagination. They sound like a call to war. With all the talk of armor and shields and breastplates, this passage of Scripture might give you the idea that the bold life in Christ is one lived on the battlefield. You can put on your armor and swing into action like Wonder Woman. If you're fierce enough, maybe you could even rock the outfit.

But when you are hurting, tired, and weak, you probably don't have the energy for a lot of heroics. You can barely lift your arms, let alone ride a horse into battle. So the whole Wonder Woman scenario falls apart quickly. And the outfit? You'll take a sweatshirt and yoga pants, thanks very much. Who fights a war in heels and a girdle anyway?

Thankfully, Paul never says you need to be a hero. He doesn't ask you to find courage within yourself. He writes, "Be strong *in the Lord* and in *his* mighty power." Maybe you thought you'd feel braver than you have. You knew life would be hard, but you didn't know it would be *this* hard. You want to feel courageous, but mostly you just feel afraid.

The world will tell you that strength is found within, but that's a muddy concept. What that usually means is that you can find it *within yourself.* This is terrible advice. It's not true. If you've been beating yourself up because you don't feel brave enough for this Midnight, you can stop. You're right. You aren't brave enough to overcome your brokenness. But you were never asked to be. To "be strong in the Lord" is to stop looking for strength within yourself altogether. It's to find it in God alone.

The armor you are told to put on in Ephesians 6 is not fashioned out of your own ability. It is God's. It's *His* truth you can trust. You walk in *His* peace. Your righteousness is only through what God has done. It is salvation given to you by *Him*. And yes, you can find amazing, fierce strength within, but it is from the Holy Spirit that lives in you.

You do not need to fight your own battles. You do not need to drum up courage. You don't even need to stop being afraid. You just need to know whose armor to put on and whose strength to rely on. Everything else is up to God.

Paul never tells us to run into battle yelling, "Charge!" To the contrary, after all his descriptions of armor, swords, and shields, his final command is somewhat anticlimactic. In the end, he tells us to stand. That's it. Stand. Not exactly Hollywood material, is it? No ninja moves required. No theatrics needed. Plant your feet firmly on the solid ground of God's strength and stand.

This is no small feat. When you are in the throes of depression or pain, standing is an incredible act of courage and faith. When you want to run or hide or at least go to Jamaica and spend all your money and not worry about the consequences, standing is everything. To stay still in your suffering means you are standing in the strength of God and trusting in His provision. It is to follow the Shepherd's lead and stay within His grasp.

The Shepherd's Song

The LORD is my shepherd, I lack nothing (Psalm 23:1).

Scholars believe David wrote Psalm 23 in the latter part of his life.[4] The reflective tone indicates someone old enough to see the past with clarity and have a quiet assurance of the future. I picture David as an old man, sitting on his throne, surrounded by all the trappings of royal life. There is nothing he cannot buy. Everything is at his fingertips. He leafs through his memories like photo album pages. He sees the wars he won and lost. He contemplates great moments of faith and the weakest times of fleshly desires. He remembers the cold feel of the cave walls and the warmth of Bathsheba's arms. Perhaps he kept his shepherd's slingshot over the years, the one he used to defeat Goliath. Maybe his fingers wrapped around it as he thought back on that first battle. I wonder if a faint smile crossed his lips as he thought about all that had taken place over the decades.

David's life held victory and defeat, love and loss, new beginnings and untimely deaths, caves, enemies, silence, joy, pain, questions, songs, heartbreak, humility, betrayal, faith, fear, and courage. David was intimately familiar with the corridors and crevices of Midnight. And near the end of his life he looked back on it all and said, "The LORD is my shepherd, I lack nothing." David knew where everything he ever needed came from.

Green Pastures

> He makes me lie down in green pastures,
> He leads me beside quiet waters,
>   he refreshes my soul (verses 2-3).

The main job of a sheep is to go where the shepherd leads. It sounds simple enough. But sheep scare easily. They startle at loud noises. They get lost. If they see one of their friends run, they run too. It doesn't matter that they don't know where they're going or why they're running. They just follow the rest of the flock. They have a variety of natural predators and their only defense mechanism is to run. Seriously. That's it. Have you seen their legs? Their only means of escaping danger are those short, stubby limbs. I'm not sure if sheep even have knees. It's funny and sad. Like when I try to sing.

To put it simply, sheep aren't the most self-reliant creatures. Their fear makes them skittish, which means it takes a while for them to learn to trust their shepherd. But over and over, they hear his voice. He calls them. He invites them. If they don't respond, he helps them along with his rod and his staff. He doesn't use his tools to beat the sheep. He uses them to direct and to protect. Over time, his voice becomes stronger than their fear. He leads them, and they follow.

The relationship between sheep and shepherd isn't reciprocal. Sheep don't have much to offer. They provide wool and some great chops, but that's about it. They can't do much of anything for themselves. They've got stout legs, a terrible sense of direction, and about 72 forms of neuroses. And yet, Jesus said, "I am the good shepherd. The good shepherd lays down his life for the sheep" (John 10:11). He died on the cross so you don't have to keep trying to be strong enough. He likes stubby legs. He put down His life so you don't have to be your own protection.

The best gift you can get is to come to the end of yourself. Midnight is an invitation to be led. To stop depending on your own strength. Are you tired of running and tired of following the mob to the next thing that leads to nothing? You are primed to hear Him. He is calling you. This Midnight has cleared the path and attuned your ears.

When you listen and respond to the leading of the Shepherd, He will take you to green pastures that will strengthen you. He will lead you beside waters that are still enough to allow you to drink all you need to quench your thirst. He will provide refreshment for your soul in ways you cannot provide for yourself. He will provide the courage you need, because He is a good Shepherd and He loves His sheep.

Right Paths

> He guides me along the right paths
> for his name's sake (verse 3).

You are not being led into and through Midnight solely for your own personal development. Yes, this journey is specifically yours. It will shape and grow your soul. It will deepen your relationship with God. But God is providing much more than that. He is leading you in paths of righteousness for *His* glory. Midnight is not yours. It's His. When you stand in His strength and His courage, people will look at you and see *Him*. When people tell you how brave and inspiring you are for walking your path with such faith, you will know none of it came from within. You will know that courage doesn't feel like it looks. You will know where you stand and you will praise His name alone.

The Darkest Valley

> Even though I walk
>   through the darkest valley,
> I will fear no evil,
>   for you are with me;
> your rod and your staff,
>   they comfort me (verse 4).

It makes perfect sense to be afraid of Midnight. To be stripped of self-reliance is disorienting. To have scads of predators and only semi-functioning knees is upsetting. You are defenseless. If you didn't know that before, this refining process is making it abundantly clear. The good news is that you don't need to provide your own defense. He's leading the way and your main job, your only job, is to stay in His presence.

You are going to bump up against His rod and staff. They might even bruise you. You can trust them because you can trust the Shepherd. They are keeping you from going off a cliff or into a ravine. They are not there to beat you into submission or break your spirit. They are keeping you on the path. Scripture tells you how to follow

Him. If you are letting His Word penetrate your soul and influence your life, you're going to feel it, most of all when the Word of God pokes and prods you. If you never experience the painful push of the Shepherd's rod, you're not letting Him lead.

A Table Before Me

> You prepare a table before me
>   in the presence of my enemies.
> You anoint my head with oil;
>   my cup overflows (verse 5).

David often talks about his enemies in his psalms. There were real armies after him. Bad guys who had swords and carried shields and didn't use dental floss. They wanted to kill David. They were not nice. It's no surprise David asked God to destroy them.

As far as I know, I don't have enemies like that. There are people who do not like me. There are people who have done things to hurt me. Some of those people love Jesus too. Are they my enemy? Aren't we both God's children? I suspect so. I get a bit uneasy when I try to define other people as enemies (at least the ones who aren't chasing me down with a sword!). Anne Lamott said, "You can safely assume that you've created God in your own image when it turns out that God hates all the same people you do."[5] I try to stay out of the "he's my enemy" business.

Hopefully, you're not surrounded by flesh-and-blood humans out to destroy your life. If so, put down this book and call 911 immediately. But most of us are not in that situation. Nonetheless, we *do* have enemies: despair, temptation, hopelessness, self-pity. They *are* after us. I'm pretty sure none of them use dental floss either.

It used to be a sign of great respect to anoint a guest's head with oil. I doubt any dinner guest in the twenty-first century would enjoy this, however. But back in biblical times, it was more than just a sign of hospitality, it meant honor. Remember the story of the woman who anointed Jesus's feet with oil? One of the reasons she was criticized was because her actions were unbelievably extravagant. Judas considered it wasteful (John 12:4). So much expensive oil running over one man's feet, flowing into the cracks of the floor, pooling everywhere like it wasn't as precious as it was. It was dripping like a faucet, streaming forth, and seemed over the top, outrageous, and even obscene.

Midnight is the table before you. It is set in the presence of your enemies: doubt, depression, maybe even self-hatred. The enemy of your soul has pulled up a chair next to you and is telling you over and over again that you are weak. That you are failing at this faith walk. That you are a disappointment and a disaster. He will keep talking. He will not shut up. But his is not the only voice. You are not alone with him. The good Shepherd is here too. He is the One who has prepared this place. He has been expecting you. He is inviting you to sit here and rest. The company is uncomfortably mixed. This isn't a tea party. It's more like those Thanksgiving dinners when all the relatives come over, weird Uncle Al is getting drunk at one end of the table, and Aunt Sally is ranting about politics at the other. It doesn't really matter though. In the midst of the crazy, you have a place. There is a soft chair and a clean plate waiting for you. A napkin, fork, knife, and spoon are set. Everything you need is here. A banquet awaits. While the guests around rant and rave and create madness, the Shepherd is preparing a decanter of oil. It is full and rich and warm. Slowly and with great care, He pours His precious oil over you. You can feel it flow over your face and down your neck. It runs through your hair, drips down your forehead, and rolls over the sides of your cheeks. You feel the oil pool inside your ears. It fills them, muffling the sounds of the enemy and his accusations. The warmth of the oil is comforting and soft. It relaxes your shoulders and soothes your tired body. You are consumed by its fragrance. It is shaping you even as it envelops the shape of your body. It sinks deep into your pores.

If you've been waiting to feel brave in this season, you don't need to wait anymore. Courage isn't the antidote to fear anyway. First John 4:18 says that "perfect love drives out fear." Love is already with you, anointing your head and filling your cup. Courage comes from being loved beyond measure. And you are.

You will know deep in your soul that God's strength is enough when you stop trying to be strong all by yourself. His strength is precious oil splashing over you, pouring out and seeping into the cracks of your heart. Even in the darkest valleys, it is overflowing. You have all you need and more. You can trust Him with your weakness; it is where you will find your greatest strength.

All the Days of My Life

> Surely your goodness and love will follow me
>   all the days of my life,
> and I will dwell in the house of the LORD
>   forever (verse 6).

It was a gigantic hunk of marble weighing well over six tons. It was quite a feat to make the 88-mile trip from where it was mined in the Italian town of Carrara to Florence. In 1463, sculptor Agostino di Duccio was commissioned to create a statue of David that would be displayed on a buttress of the Florence cathedral. He quickly got to work but didn't get very far before he was off the project completely. Only the roughest suggestion of a torso and legs could be seen in the massive allotment. For the next 37 years, this enormous, expensive piece of marble sat in the cathedral yard, turned on its back, ignored and exposed to the elements. When an inventory of the cathedral warehouse was done in 1500, it was noted that "a certain figure of marble called David, badly blocked out and supine" was among the conglomeration of assets.[6]

The building committee decided to undertake the David project again. This time, they hired a 26-year-old artist named Michelangelo. It took him three years to complete. From its first unveiling in September 1504, the sculpture was seen as a breathtaking work of art.

The story of David and Goliath was a popular one among artists during this period. Renaissance art always depicted David at the height of his strength, victorious over Goliath. Sometimes he was shown just as he was about to cut off Goliath's head, other times he's holding it victoriously in his hand. Always with Goliath. Always a winner.[7]

But Michelangelo's statue was different from the usual interpretation. He shows David *before* he fights Goliath. He's not brandishing a sword. He hasn't won anything yet. He is holding a rock and a slingshot. Are those even considered weapons? They are definitely less exciting than a sword and decapitation. Surely not as heroic. Moreover, in Michelangelo's depiction, David is naked. He's there in all his splendor—without even a fig leaf. I'm sure you've seen a photo of this famous work. The first time you saw it, you may have even giggled. Especially if you were in junior high and you found a photo of it in the school library. David is ready for battle, but lacks everything required for a fair fight, including underwear. And yet his face reveals steely determination. He is prepared. He is equipped. David doesn't need anything more than a stone and a sling. Goliath doesn't matter. The Lord is his Shepherd. David lacks nothing.

The Gift of Courage

> Courage is more exhilarating than fear and in the long
> run it is easier. We do not have to become heroes over-
> night. Just a step at a time, meeting each thing that comes
> up, seeing it is not as dreadful as it appeared, discovering
> we have the strength to stare it down.
>
> —ELEANOR ROOSEVELT[8]

The gift of courage is that fear doesn't own you. God does. The armor you wear is the truth of His love, His provision, His power. You cannot be defeated. Goodness and mercy have followed you all the days of your life. They will continue to do so. The winds will rage. You will take on water. Panic will rise. Anxiety will rush into your heart. But it's in the center of the storm that courage is born, because Jesus is there too. When love is present, fear's grip loosens. The gift of courage is that you can *fear not* even when you are afraid. In the sallow pit of Midnight, He is restoring your soul, calling you to a faith that is deeper than your doubts and stronger than your fear.

The gift of courage is that you are not required to produce it. It's the result of being loved in your weakness. It's what you get when you trust in the love of God for your defense. It is the unmovable assurance that you are enough because He is enough. As David's most famous psalm reflects, it is the by-product of a lifetime in the Shepherd's care.

To trust this over the top, outrageous love that spills over your feet and into the cracks on the floor is the bravest thing you can do. It is to declare freedom from fear even when you are scared. The grace of courage is suiting up for battle and discovering that the war is already won. You have everything you need and more because you already have the Shepherd. You can stand in His love. You can stand in His provision. You can stand in His strength. You can stand.

MOONLIGHT MEDITATIONS

- What do you believe, deep down in your soul, about God?
- What stories have you made up about God that come from fear?
- In what areas of your life do you long for courage?
- How is this Midnight maturing your faith?

EVENING STROLL

- Write a list of the areas in your life where you seek courage. For example:

  o I need courage to _____

  o I need courage in my relationship with

  _____

- Once you are done, go over your list a second time and write *My Shepherd's love* in place of the word "courage" or "courageous" (for example, I need ~~courage~~ *My Shepherd's love* to…).
- Looking at your list, let it sink in that you have all that you need right now, even if you feel afraid. Go over your list again. This time, replace the word "need" with "have." Say this out loud.
- Allow it to become your song of praise to the Shepherd (for example, I ~~need~~ *have* my Shepherd's love to…).

9

WAITING FOR THE SUN TO RISE

Hope is being able to see that there is light despite all of the darkness.

DESMOND TUTU[1]

I don't remember much from when my kids were newborns. It was all such a blur in those first few months. However, I do remember the evening of January 16, 1994, with clarity. Danny and I were living in Huntington Beach, California. Our first child, Elizabeth, was born in December, so we were in the dizzying trenches of new parenthood. That night I visited the home of my parents in Granada Hills, a suburb about an hour away from where Danny and I lived.

Elizabeth was born premature and weighed only about six pounds by then. A crib or playpen seemed to swallow her up, so we lined a dresser drawer with blankets and padding and let her sleep there instead. That night I went to sleep in my parents' guest bedroom, with Elizabeth in the drawer on the floor next to me.

At 4:30 a.m., we were jolted awake by an earthquake so severe it felt like someone was shaking a snow globe with us in it. I was knocked out of bed and landed over the drawer where Elizabeth was sleeping. It was pitch black and things were falling down all around me. The noise was deafening, not just from everything crashing to the floor, but from the rollicking earth itself. The shaking was so violent it was impossible to get to my feet or run for safety. All I could do was cover my head and shield my daughter with my body.

Once the quaking stopped, the house went silent. The combined odors of Worcester, soy sauce, cooking wine, and salad dressing was overpowering. The contents of the now-opened and tilted refrigerator were broken open all over the floor. My parents and I called out to one another, assuring each other we were all in one piece. We carefully shuffled out of the house and into the cool air of the night, barefoot and in our pajamas. Elizabeth slept through the whole thing.

When we had our bearings, my dad went back into the house and somehow found his car keys near the front door. We got in the car and drove to my brother's home nearby. He and his wife were thankfully safe and sound too. Because the power was out, we were surrounded by pitch dark. No one could assess the damage or go back into their homes. Glass was everywhere, furniture was tossed, and there were too many hazards to make any decisions. We sat in the car, turned on the radio, and listened to the news.

We learned that the epicenter of the Northridge earthquake was a mere five miles from my parents' home. The authorities were telling people to stay put and not to drive anywhere as freeways were collapsed, leaking gas lines were exploding, household pets were running loose, and there was untold damage all around. The news told us the sun was set to rise at 7:00 a.m. Until then we needed to stay where we were. It was unsafe to do anything else. So there we sat, shaken, confused, and counting the minutes until the sun would rise.

I've always loved sunrises. They always come. They're always beautiful. But until January 17, 1994, I never *needed* a sunrise. I'd never waited for the exact moment I could expect to see the sun peek over the horizon. Between 4:30 a.m. and 7:00 a.m. that day, darkness held us captive. We knew the light would come. We were even lucky enough to know *when* it would come. But it wasn't there yet.

Hating Hope

I used to hate hope. Every so often, it would rise up in me for one reason or another, only to fade over time or be altogether crushed. There were so many things I hoped for: better relationships, a clearer sense of direction, a thicker skin (one where my feelings would not be hurt so often), better looks, and a better body. Most of all I hoped depression would leave me once and for all. It's not like I was expecting to be walking on sunshine every day. I knew life wasn't a never-ending birthday party with balloons and cake. I just wanted to feel like I had a grip. I was so tired of debilitating, undefined sadness that returned again and again. I wanted to feel normal.

There were seasons that made me believe this was possible. I would experience months, even years without the daunting effects of deep depression. Sure, I would get sad or anxious or have blue days like anyone else. But they would lift. And they didn't make me feel like I was going to die. I would begin to believe the stake in my flesh was finally gone and my hope was realized. Then, out of nowhere and often without reason, it would return, pulling me into its deep waters of despair. Depression is like drowning without dying. So often, it would carry me away, and I would lose sight of the shore once more. Hope would recede into the darkness.

I remember writing in my journal "I HATE HOPE." I would rather have not hoped at all than see it dismantled before my eyes. I blamed hope for making me imagine a life without the darkness. I blamed hope for making me vulnerable enough to believe things could change. I felt hope betray me again and again. No wonder I hated it. Perhaps you have wanted something for as long as you can remember, and you've been disappointed so many times that you hate hope too.

Over time I discovered that it wasn't hope I'd been relying on. I'd mistaken it for something else. When I prayed for my depression to leave once and for all, it was a prayer born out of deep longing. It was *desire*. I wanted it to go. I believed I needed it to go. I could not see any way to survive and thrive while it circled around my head and heart. It was a sincere prayer uttered in desperation, born of the belief that I knew what my own life needed most. In retrospect, I can see now that my hope was in the prayer itself, not in the One to whom I was praying. It is a critical distinction.

Imitation Hope

Like a nice Chanel bag, hope has a lot of imitators. Until we inspect it up close, look at the seams, and study the stitching, hope will look a lot like desires, wishes, or longings. Most of us use the words "hope" and "want" like they mean the same thing.

"I want sushi for dinner tonight."

"I hope my son will call."

"I want my marriage to survive."

"I hope this sushi is fresh."

It might sound like splitting hairs, but there is an essential difference between hoping and longing.

Longings are what you want but may not actually get. They run the gamut from the superficial to the profound. You can long for cancer to disappear or you can long for a new patio set. You can wish for a better marriage or a better golf game. Longings vary in depth and detail, but they all arise out of desire for something to change. They are formulated in response to the very normal human desire to find relief from want, from pain, from lack of control. Wishes, longings, desires—whatever you call them—they are all dependent upon a shift of circumstance to be satisfied.

I imagined that if my depression disappeared, I would finally be okay. I could manage my life without feeling defeated by it. If the things that haunted me finally left, I believed I would find the freedom I'd been searching for. I held out for healing and called it hope.

To believe our longings will fulfill our deepest needs is like hooking up a Chihuahua to a dogsled and expecting to get somewhere. They just aren't built to pull that much weight. This doesn't mean they are useless or superficial. Longings are real and important. Desires matter to God. Confessing our needs and wants will help to develop intimacy with God. It's not trite or presumptuous to declare what we want. There are countless examples in Scripture where faithful people prayed for their longings to be met. David prayed for victory. Hannah prayed for a child. Paul prayed to see his friends in Thessalonica. All kinds of people asked Jesus for healing. These were significant things to ask. These were life-altering requests. They all turned to God with their desires.

I suspect about 90 percent of my prayers are made up of my desires and longings. I don't know what I'd pray about if I didn't have a laundry list of ways I think things should go. I've always imagined that God really wants my input, like He's waiting for me to weigh in before making the big decisions. So I prattle on about everything that flurries around my mind. I make key suggestions about what I am hoping for in the lives of my kids, my husband, and my friends. I don't leave anything out. He knows it's all inside of me anyway. Why pretend I'm only concerned with world peace when He knows full well I can't stop thinking about the headache I've had all afternoon that is probably nothing but could be a brain tumor?

Asking God for anything takes guts. You never know how He

will respond. Ask anyway. Ask God for everything you long for, wish, desire, or just plain want. Ask Him for the big and the small, the grandiose and the minute. Tell Him about the yearnings that make you feel like you might die if you don't get them and the wishes that disappear like smoke a day after they emerge. Mention the stuff that is embarrassingly trite, like a parking space or a good hair day. Confess your deepest longings even when it terrifies you to do so. Your relationship with God will deepen and widen with every spoken desire. The things your heart aches for will bring you to the feet of God, which makes them vital to your relationship with Him. But don't wait for your longings to fulfill your deepest needs. They can't deliver on that. They are signposts pointing the way, but they are not the destination. While they are born out of sincere (and sometimes not-so-sincere) desires and developed by legitimate (and not-so-legitimate) human needs, they cannot offer what your soul craves most. Only hope can do that.

No Matter What

God isn't one to draw inside the lines. He doesn't seem to be a big fan of the predictable or even logical—at least by human standards. It's not His style. He looks at the lines and laughs. Then He draws outside those lines like a three-year-old hopped up on Pixy Stix and holding a purple crayon. He revels in coloring outside the margins. And off the page. And all over the table. And on to the floor. And up the walls. The difference is that every mark God makes is intentional and deliberate.

No, He's not one to draw inside the lines. His power and plans are too big for any of us to anticipate. So it's not surprising if you are angry or confused by what God is doing in your life. This isn't necessarily a bad thing. It can be the start of something new.

To let go of all you thought God would do in your life is the beginning of powerful, resilient hope that cannot be shaken no matter how dark it gets.

To hope is to love God like David did. His relationship with God was as tumultuous as it was intimate. Because David loved God so profoundly, he was saddened, confused, and surprised regularly. Deep love invites deep hurt. Only those you trust most have the ability to wound you to your core. A stranger on the street or a mere acquaintance might be able to harm you, but never in the same way as those you love with all your heart. Intimacy always includes vulnerability. And vulnerability means risk. To risk loving God the way David did is to open yourself up to disappointment and disillusionment.

> In you, LORD my God,
>   I put my trust.
> I trust in you;
>   do not let me be put to shame,
>   nor let my enemies triumph over me.
> No one who hopes in you
>   will ever be put to shame (Psalm 25:1-3).

David's faith in God was evident from the time he grabbed that slingshot and stone, stood toe-to-toe with Goliath, and didn't blink. Even so, David's feelings toward God were all over the map. His words are black-and-white manifestations of what it looks like when hope is forged, refined, and shaped by a vulnerable life with God.

Though he always had faith, I believe David's *hope* was developed and matured over time. As we said in chapter 2, suffering is the conduit to intimacy with God. He needed the deep wounds of unmet desires to strip away his expectations of what the Lord would do with his life. David's faith may have always been in his heart, but I suspect his hope was developed most acutely through the experience of suffering.

Romans 5:2-5 states, "We boast in the hope of the glory of God. Not only so, but we also glory in our sufferings, because we know that suffering produces perseverance; perseverance, character; and character, hope. And hope does not put us to shame, because God's love has been poured out into our hearts through the Holy Spirit, who has been given to us." Please note that these verses do not say that suffering *itself* produces hope. I cannot think of one example where pain produces immediate and satisfactory pleasure. It takes months in the gym for flab to turn to muscle. A college degree takes years. Even childbirth, perhaps the most intensely painful experience connected to the most incredible outcome, requires recovery time. Sure, once that baby is out, your body no longer feels like it's being split in two by a medieval torture device, but it's sure not ready for a marathon. It requires a time of mending, building, and strengthening. Most of the time, you are not going to move straight from suffering to hope. But it will bring you a step closer to it. Pain will produce perseverance.

My daughter, Elizabeth, has developmental delays. Her disabilities run the gamut, but one of her most pronounced attributes is that she repeats herself. She talks about the same things. I've heard stories about horses and kittens every day of my life for at least 15 years. This might seem cute as you read this. It might bring a smile to your face because it's so sweet. But please understand that I am not exaggerating. Day in. Day out. Every month. Every year. Kittens and horses. Horses and kittens. Not even new stories about kittens and horses. The same ones. Over and over and over again. There are days when I truly feel like I am going to lose my ever-lovin' mind. But I've got to admire Elizabeth's persistence. That girl has it in spades. She just keeps talking. And I love her so much it hurts. So as long as she keeps talking, I will keep listening. Somewhere in the unfathomable number of repeated stories, Elizabeth's persistence has developed mine.

David asked God for all kinds of things: to defeat his enemies, restore his passion, rescue him from danger, and to stop his suffering. He let all his longings be known. Sometimes God gave David what he wanted. Sometimes He didn't. Either way, David kept talking. With every declaration of fear, courage, desire, sin, sadness, doubt, and faith, David reached out to God. Over and over again. Even when he was not sure God was listening, he plowed ahead. Just as Romans 5:3-5 states, his suffering produced dogged perseverance. And it led him back, over and over again, to the One who would not leave.

David's identity was shaped and sharpened when he turned his heart toward God. Every time David looked for God, he found God looking at him. He could tell the same stories of uncertainty and fear, and the Lord never even came close to losing His ever-lovin' mind. He just kept loving David. David's persistence revealed God's consistency. In turn, it shaped his identity. Every encounter with God assured David he was not alone. There was nothing he could do to make God turn away. He knew his Lord would be there every single time. Over and over again. It became the defining aspect of David's character. He was the one after God's own heart. He *knew* God was present with him. And because David had God, he had unshakable hope. It wasn't a longing. It wasn't a feeling. It was a *knowing* that transcended emotion, circumstance, and even the darkest Midnights.

When David saw Bathsheba bathing on the roof, he let his longings take over and his desire rule the day. He didn't go to God with his desires. He went straight down the rabbit hole of lust, envy, and pride. He committed adultery and murder because his unconfessed longing mutated into immediate, fleshly, burning need. When the prophet Nathan held a mirror up to his behavior, David was overwhelmed by what he saw. He was filled with remorse over his disobedience toward the God he loved. During this time, Bathsheba gave birth to a baby boy, born as a result of David's unscrupulous behavior. But the child was not healthy. For a solid week, David fasted and prayed and begged God to heal his son. David made the mistake of keeping his longings to himself earlier. He wasn't going to do it again. He was going to lay down at the feet of his Abba and declare his longings over and over again.

On the seventh day it was over. "When David saw his servants whispering, he knew that the baby was dead. So he asked them, 'Is the baby dead?' They answered, 'Yes, he is dead.' Then David got up from the floor, washed himself, put lotions on, and changed his clothes. Then he went into the LORD's house to worship" (2 Samuel 12:19-20 NCV).

For seven days, David did nothing but pour out his heart to God. He pleaded with God to spare his son's life. David grieved over his sin and confessed his sorrow. The Lord allowed David's son to die anyway. How did David respond? He worshipped. It's incredible. It's mind-blowing. It's almost incomprehensible. And it is a breathtaking demonstration of the hope David had in God. It was a hope that allowed for unabashed nakedness before the Lord and complete trust when the worst happened. David's sorrow was palpable, his grief overwhelming. And yet his hope in God remained unshakable.

David was born brave, ready to take on lions and giants. But he didn't trust in his strength. He was anointed by God to be the king of Israel. But he didn't hope in his destiny. He was wealthy beyond measure. He didn't rely on his riches. He was victorious in battles. He didn't trust in his wits. David placed his hope wholly and completely in God alone. He knew it was the only safe place for his hope to live. He knew Abba was there, had been there, and would be with him always. David had hope because David had God. No matter what, God was with him.

Shame and Hope

In Psalm 25, David says that no one who hopes in God will be put to shame. In Romans 5:5, Paul tells us something similar. Both men contrast shame and hope as opposites. But if hope has the overall meaning of optimism and shame means something like embarrassment or guilt, then why do David and Paul contrast them? Wouldn't pessimism be the opposite of hope? Wouldn't pride be a better contrast to shame? What does hope have to do with shame in the first place? To understand the connection, let's go back to paradise.

In the beginning, Adam and Eve walked around the garden of Eden in perfect relationship with God, each other, and themselves. God was in charge and He provided everything. Adam was a stud. Eve walked around naked and never once worried about whether or not her thighs jiggled. Neither doubted God's goodness and love. Trust was complete. Then it all changed with one conversation. Here's how it went down:

> Now the serpent was more crafty than any of the wild animals the LORD God had made. He said to the woman, "Did God really say, 'You must not eat from any tree in the garden'?"
>
> The woman said to the serpent, "We may eat fruit from the trees in the garden, but God did say, 'You must not eat fruit from the tree that is in the middle of the garden, and you must not touch it, or you will die.'"
>
> "You will not certainly die," the serpent said to the woman. "For God knows that when you eat from it your eyes will be opened, and you will be like God, knowing good and evil."

> When the woman saw that the fruit of the tree was good for food and pleasing to the eye, and also desirable for gaining wisdom, she took some and ate it. She also gave some to her husband, who was with her, and he ate it. Then the eyes of both of them were opened, and they realized they were naked; so they sewed fig leaves together and made coverings for themselves (Genesis 3:1-6).

You can almost hear the condescending, snide tone in which Satan asks her, "Did God *actually* say…" Kind of like when I say to Danny as we are leaving for a dinner party, "Are you *actually* planning to wear that hideous shirt?" Poor guy. There's not much room for a fair exchange of ideas on fashion and personal taste when I put it like that.

Satan's question implied the answer. He was suggesting that God was holding out on them, and because of that, God was not to be trusted. For the first time in her life, Eve doubted the goodness of her Creator. That God was in control was no longer a reassurance. Now it made Eve uneasy. She felt a pang of incompleteness. She started to believe that God was withholding something from her that she desperately needed. So she decided to take matters into her own hands, take a bite, and swallow.

The first thing Adam and Eve realized after their fateful decision was that they were naked. Until then, it wasn't a thing. But now? They were exposed. Vulnerable. Jiggly. "So they sewed fig leaves together and made coverings for themselves." They decided on their own what should be covered up and what could stay exposed. They hid their bodies and then they hid from God altogether.

Brené Brown wrote, "Shame is the fear of disconnection—it's the fear that something we've done or failed to do, an ideal that we've not lived up to, or a goal that we've not accomplished makes us unworthy of connection."[2] Adam and Eve failed. But it was they who hid from God—not the other way around.

Being that shame is the "fear of disconnection," as Brown asserts, it's ironic that shame serves as a powerful source of separation. Shame breaks, shatters, and produces edgy shards that scatter across the floor. Shame disconnects us from ourselves, one another, and, most important, God. If this is its effect, then the antidote to such separation is found in Jesus Christ. Jesus heals and redeems and resurrects. He doesn't just bring hope. Jesus *is* hope. His entire purpose for coming to earth, dying on the cross, and resurrecting from the grave was to invite us into relationship with God. No more separation. No more hiding. No more shame. No matter how much you mess up. No matter how messed up you are. Jesus has ensured you will always be in relationship with your Creator. You will never be alone. He is the manifestation of all that your soul both longs for and needs. Romans 8:1-2 declares, "Therefore, there is now no condemnation for those who are in Christ Jesus, because through Christ Jesus the law of the Spirit who gives life has set you free from the law of sin and death." In Jesus Christ there is no shame, because there is no separation from Him. This is the truest hope there is.

Unshaken

Some people assume hope is strictly for heaven. Or for the second coming of Jesus. Or at least they've regarded it as what you do when you're waiting for something you don't have. Those thoughts are accurate. When you've placed your hope in Jesus Christ, you are assured that heaven will be your home. First John 5:13 says, "I write these things to you who believe in the name of the Son of God so that you may know that you have eternal life." Someday in the future you will not struggle with sadness or suffering. There will be no more tears. You will be in the presence of the One who loves you more than you can imagine. You can hope for heaven because it is promised by God. Heaven is not just wishful thinking. You might not have seen it yet, but it's a genuine place.

And yet the hope of heaven isn't much comfort when you feel like your eyes are bleeding out of your head from crying so much. It's like that bumper sticker on a rusted-out Ford that says "Don't let my car fool you, my real treasure is in heaven." One has little to do with the other. I don't think having a run-down car means you have stronger faith. It just means you have a crappy car. I firmly believe the only lasting treasures are in heaven, but I'd still like to get to the grocery store without having to call a tow truck.

Heaven can be a flimsy reassurance when you are enveloped by Midnight. It's just too far away to bring much comfort. When you're suffering, the idea of heaven might be enough for eternity, but it's hardly enough to make it through the night.

Thankfully, there is more to hope than heaven. Hope is not just for "someday" when your circumstances aren't so bad and the pain isn't so excruciating. Hope is the "not yet" and also the "now." It's coming and it's already here. Jesus made it possible for hope to be just as powerful in the present as it is for the future. His Holy Spirit dwells in you right now. He has made His home in you and He won't move out. Like David, you can cry out, lament, doubt, and fear. God is here. You can mourn, grieve, fall silent, or scream aloud. God will remain. The darkness can come and threaten to take you away, but God will not let you go.

Hope isn't reliant upon circumstances, which means it can't be beaten down or thwarted easily. Unlike longings or desires, hope doesn't need a change in situation to be realized. It shows up smack dab in the middle of crazy and sets up shop. It will not bend to circumstance. Hope will not be pushed around by naysayers. It refuses to be affected by bad odds and cannot be tempered by affliction.

Hope is built and emboldened in the depths of Midnight because it is planted in the soil of suffering. Hope isn't afraid to get messy. Hope is rebellious. Hope is defiant.

The difficulty of hope is the same as its best feature: It isn't reliant on circumstances. Therefore, it may not shift your situation in the least. If you're hoping hope will get you out of your mess, you're hoping up the wrong tree. It might not remove your suffering one iota. But because hope is as real as Jesus Christ Himself, the darkest Midnight and the deepest pain cannot kill it. Ever. Just as suffering produces perseverance and perseverance creates character and character builds hope, so the suffering of Midnight will bring about a hope that remains unshaken in the face of despair.

No Missing Pieces

I prayed over and over again for God to take away my deepest afflictions. When it did not happen, I doubted God's goodness. Like Eve, I wondered if He was holding out on me. Like a puzzle from a garage sale, I was sure I was missing pieces. It was devastating to feel that damaged. It felt like God was keeping the best blessings to Himself or giving them to other people instead.

But the most vulnerable parts of your personhood and the most painful aspects of your story are not a result of God's frugality. Eve was just as naked before she ate the fruit as she was after. Her vulnerability and nakedness were not liabilities; they were intentional and beautiful in the eyes of God. They were there before everything went south, which means they were never a problem that needed solving. Just because she didn't know as much as God didn't mean she was lacking in anything. She was whole because she was His.

Satan crept in and whispered stories of God's scarcity while surrounded by His abundance. The garden of Eden was overflowing with trees heavy with fruit. Eve had access to everything she needed and more. She wasn't missing any pieces. Her vulnerability was only a problem when she trusted herself more than she trusted God. Shame only made an appearance after she believed she needed more than she had. When she hid from God, she hid from hope.

I prayed for God to take away the stake in my side for a long time. So far, He has not. I've made peace with that. I no longer place my hope in my prayers; I place them in the One I pray to. I don't hate my weaknesses anymore. I've started to trust their meaning and value because I've started to trust my meaning and value in the eyes of God. Vulnerability in the presence of hope is nothing to be ashamed of.

Some of your longings may never be fulfilled. That will probably always sting a little. But you will perpetually have what you need most. God does not withhold His abundance, because He does not withhold Himself.

Confess the wishes you have for your life. Then release the expectations you've held for their answers. Let your deepest desires slip through your fingers in order to hold on to something more powerful. Open your hand wide and grasp the hope that Jesus Christ offers instead, namely, His unshakable presence in the midst of Midnight. He may not give you all that you ask or want. But He will give what you need most with abundance, because He gives Himself with abandon. Emotions, longings, and circumstances will shift and swirl. Weaknesses and failings will emerge. In all of them, Jesus Christ remains unmovable. Hope is the foundation upon which you can build your life. You are not missing any pieces. You will not be put to shame.

Placing your hope in God isn't some wispy, romantic idea that floats around in shades of pastel and glimmers of craft glue. It is a bold, brave act. It declares once and for all that your circumstances do not have the final say. Hope has the final word because God has the final word. It's not just for someday. Hope is right here. Right now.

The Gift of Hope

> And that was what Job needed above all else—not an explanation of suffering, but the revelation that even in the midst of suffering there is a God who is with us and for us and will never let us go.
>
> —FREDERICK BUECHNER[3]

We sat in my father's car on that dark, early morning of January 17, 1994. Mom, dad, me, and my newborn baby. My brother and his wife stood next to the car. Aftershocks from the earthquake rocked us every few minutes. We were disoriented and afraid. Our conversation was rambling and filled with speculation about what the next few hours would reveal. We didn't know much, but we knew the sun would rise. Everything else was up for grabs. But the sun would absolutely emerge. We could be assured of that. We were counting the minutes until it did.

Hope works in the darkness. In the silence, in the aftershocks of divorce, death, and suffering, hope is reliable. The gift of hope is that it will absolutely, positively emerge. Like the sun, hope is never truly gone, even when you can't see it. Hope will always rise. You don't need to manufacture it. You don't need to drum it up. Hope already exists.

The gift of hope is that you do not need to see any evidence of morning in order to believe there is one. You can trust that something is happening even when nothing is happening. God is always at work. He brings redemption to your past, refinement to your present, and restoration to your future. Hope is here because He is here.

Hope will never put you to shame because there is no condemnation in Christ Jesus. Shame cannot live where He is. To stand in His presence is to stand naked and vulnerable in the presence of hope.

In the radiance of Jesus's presence, shame will retreat into the shadows. It might shout or whisper accusations toward you about your incompleteness, your unlovability, or your lack. Shame might tell you lies about God's cruelty or His stinginess. You don't need to listen.

Although the Lord may not always answer your prayers in the way you desire, He is steadfastly answering your deepest needs. He offers you a hope that shines in the darkest places because He offers you His presence. He will never leave you. He will never forsake you. You will not be alone for one moment. In Him alone you can place your trust. And when morning breaks and the sun finally begins to shine again, He will be there too. You've got hope because you have Jesus. He will not let you go.

MOONLIGHT MEDITATIONS

- What longings do you have that feel more like needs?

- Do you trust that God is with you in this Midnight? Why or why not?

- What do you hope for in the future?

- Where do you need to experience the presence of God most right now?

EVENING STROLL

- Make a list of your longings. Write as many as you can think of, from the trite to the important. Even the ones that are embarrassing or would not be good for you. For each one, confess to God your desires. Allow yourself the vulnerability of asking. Trust Him with your yearnings. Ask Him to reveal His presence in these specific areas.

- Make a list of the things you are most grateful for in this season. These are signs of God's abundance even in the dark places. Allow gratitude to saturate your soul. Praise Him for all He provides.

WELCOME TO DAYLIGHT

To be grateful for an unanswered prayer, to give thanks in a
state of interior desolation, to trust in the love of God in the
face of the marvels, cruel circumstances, obscenities, and
commonplaces of life is to whisper a doxology in the darkness.

BRENNAN MANNING[1]

The dark places have gifts the light cannot offer. They come wrapped in tears and heartache, but they open up into an abundance of intimacy and healing. They'll probably never be anyone's favorite season of life. Sunlight will always feel warmer than the cool of evening. When we stop dreading Midnight and embrace it instead, we allow God's acceptance of us to become our own. We can make friends with the parts of our story we've despised.

Midnight is a lesson in what God provides when you've got nothing left. It will allow you to stop relying on yourself. Midnight will invite you into need and longing. It will teach you vulnerability and weakness. Midnight will show the way of silence and white space. To the uninitiated, this might sound awful. These aspects of Midnight will appear as things to be avoided. But you're learning the way of the dark night of the soul. You're beginning to understand the nature of strength found in weakness. You're experiencing the faith that springs out of doubt. You're starting to trust the presence of God even when He is silent. You now believe that Midnight has a radiance all its own.

Maybe you're no longer looking for daylight at all. Perhaps you've gotten quite comfortable here. You've learned to be content in the uncertainty of the unknown. You've explored the deepest wounds of your life and discovered they contain gifts of beauty and grace. You've walked the dark path of Midnight and you've been changed. You know that the darkness has more to offer than pain. No wonder you aren't ready to leave just yet. Maybe you like a smaller, quieter world. Maybe you're not ready for the light and the noise and an increase of activity. Maybe you don't want people to expect something from you so soon.

It's understandable. Once you discover the blessings of Midnight, it's hard to want to leave them. The quiet intimacy with Abba forged in desperation and pain is precious. But you won't need to leave it behind. The gifts of a dark place can be brought with you into the sun. You are not made to stay in the darkness. You are meant to live a full and beautiful life of purpose, relationship, and adventure. You belong to more than just the night. You belong to the daylight too. You belong to your whole life in all its fullness, pain, and glory.

Your daylight work has kept for some time now. Your gifts and talents are waiting for you. When you're ready, you can pick them up one at a time. You can slowly explore and rediscover them. They may not look the same as when you set them down. Running into your limitations has taught you quite a bit. Some things will have changed so much you no longer want them. Other aspects of your life will become more precious than ever. You will have the privilege of missing aspects of yourself and welcoming them back home.

You will not be the same person who entered into Midnight.

At least, I hope you won't be. The gifts are too abundant and profound not to be changed by them. Midnight was created to make an impact. You've walked by faith, not by sight, and it is shaping your soul. You might be quieter than before. You might be less frantic. Your world might be smaller than it was. But that will all be okay with you, because Midnight is teaching you to be content even when everything is stripped away.

Jesus has invited us to follow Him farther and deeper into the faith journey. He is showing us the way, even if it's one dimly lit step at a time. The importance of Midnight is never rushed. It's as much a time of slow healing as it is sacred wounding. It brings us to the end of our self so we can experience where Jesus begins.

To understand God's grace in all circumstances is too great a gift to remain in the darkness.

The purpose of Midnight is to bring it with you into the daylight. The blessings you've discovered in this time are effective in both the darkness and the light. You might not be prepared for the brightness just yet. But eventually you will be. You are created for daylight too. God will lead you there when you're ready.

Morning doesn't so much appear as it *unfolds*. Much like the onset of Midnight, it is so gradual, you can't pinpoint its exact arrival. All you'll know is that one day it's there. Little by little, daylight will come. And you will begin to feel the sunlight on your face once more.

Known

> You have searched me, LORD,
>   and you know me.
> You know when I sit and when I rise;
>   you perceive my thoughts from afar.
> You discern my going out and my lying down;
>   you are familiar with all my ways (Psalm 139:1-3).

In spite of David's emotional spin cycle, the Lord chose him to be king. He knew what David's story would involve. He saw the victories and defeats. He knew David would live in both caves and castles. He understood David would be capable of both great faith and great sin. Nevertheless, his weaknesses did not dampen God's affection.

David was chosen, called, and anointed by God when he was still very young. He was picked for greatness. And yet the road to greatness was blanketed in Midnight. Not once, not twice, but over and over again David experienced times of brilliant light and suffocating darkness. Over and over again he called out to God. Over and over again God answered. It wasn't always in ways David expected or wanted. But the Lord was always there. He never left David's side even when David couldn't feel His presence. God *knew* David. And it was in the darkness that David learned to know God as well.

Walking by faith and not sight requires dark places. It takes stumbling around. Trust in God is matured in fear and silence, in suffering and solitude. We need the disorienting pitch of night to grow and flourish. It cannot be done any other way.

God has searched the depths of your being and He knows you more intimately than you know yourself. He has seen every weakness, every false move, and every desperate thought. He's not intimidated. He knows this darkness as well as He knows the hairs on your head and the lines on your face. He is familiar with all your ways. And He likes them. He will bring you once more into the light so you can enjoy the full radiance of His love for you. He will never leave you. He will never forsake you.

In his psalms, David wrote about darkness and light with equal fervor. He exposed us to his most admirable trust in God as well as his deepest doubts. He shared anguish and joy. He made wild proclamations and dramatic pleas. Some are inspiring. Some are embarrassing. All are vulnerable. I believe he was so achingly transparent because he trusted that God knew him better than he knew himself. If he decided the shame of dark feelings, questions, and worries were less important than the light of faith, courage, and hope, we would never be exposed to David's beautifully candid writing. And we would be less for it. I believe David would be too.

David could have cleaned up his story. He could have left out a lot of details to make himself look better. I bet it would've made God look better too—not so mysterious, not so confounding. If David cut out the hardest parts of his life, maybe God could be shrunk down into something more containable, something less wild and unpredictable. We could all calm down. We could all figure out God.

But it would not be real. It would not be true. David was bold enough to expose his story because he knew the darkness had as many gifts as the light and that God is sovereign over both. He learned to be comfortable with the uncomfortable. He was content with the mystery of God. David knew that even the darkness is light to God.

> If I say, "Surely the darkness will hide me
>   and the light become night around me,"
> even the darkness will not be dark to you;
>   the night will shine like the day,
>   for darkness is as light to you" (Psalm 139:11-12).

David offered all of himself to the Lord. David knew he did not need to fear, because even when he was scared, God would be there. In victory and agony, God would be there. In darkness and light, God would be present.

The Lord knew your Midnight before you entered into it. He was undaunted by the darkness that has terrified you. He will not let you languish in misery. He will not leave you alone in this. Whether nighttime or morning, nothing can come between you and God. And He will return daylight to your soul once more.

Joy

> For you created my inmost being;
>   you knit me together in my mother's womb.
> I praise you because I am fearfully and wonderfully made;
>   your works are wonderful,
>   I know that full well.
> My frame was not hidden from you
>   when I was made in the secret place,
>   when I was woven together in the depths of the earth.
> Your eyes saw my unformed body;
>   all the days ordained for me were written in your
>   book
>   before one of them came to be (Psalm 139:13-16).

If I decided to go with my most basic, self-protective instinct, I would not have written a book about depression. I don't want to be forever linked to the topics of dark places and deep struggle. If that is how I am seen, I doubt I'll be invited to a lot of parties, and I like parties. The last thing I want to be known as is the "Depression Lady." I never wanted this stake in my side. I don't want to be solely defined by it. But it has brought far too many gifts to distance myself from it either.

I share parts of my story at various events and retreats around the country. I am always struck by how many people have their own experience of depression, but in many cases they have never talked about it with anyone. Their stories are heartbreaking and breathtaking. Their bravery in talking about it for the first time inspires me.

But there are others who want to pray for my healing. They want God to "fix" me. Some people believe I just need enough faith and my struggle will end. Some want to clean it up, to contain it somehow. Sometimes people want to separate me from it. Once a woman commented, "I know you've struggled, but you are not your depression." I appreciated her heart, but I don't agree. It would have been more accurate to say, "Depression isn't the totality of who you are."

Depression has altered my behavior, relationships, daily schedule, perspectives, and faith. There is not an area of my life untouched by its effects. I no longer regret that. Depression *is* a part of me. It is woven throughout my story. If I treat depression like a barnacle on a ship, attached but not an actual part of me, then I deny its impact on my soul and I abandon parts of my story. In the process, I would deny parts of God's story. Because this has never been my story alone—it is His too.

Depression and anxiety bring me to dark places and difficult days, but they have also been the pathway to discovering the radiance of God's love. My weaknesses have allowed me to find the penetrating, healing, powerful grace of God. If I didn't struggle so deeply, I wouldn't need Him so much. And I want to need Him. I *need* to need Him. In trusting Jesus Christ with my vulnerabilities, I've seen His faithfulness. In questioning His plans, I've learned His goodness. In crying out to Him in the midst of suffering, I've discovered His unwavering presence. If depression were not part of me, then neither would my faith be.

I struggle and cry and need and fail and falter and fall. I am weak and strong. I doubt and have faith. I will not deny any part of myself, even the hardest ones, because God doesn't deny them either. He knit me in my mother's womb. The darkness is light to Him. Who am I to decide what is and is not necessary in my life?

I've wandered around the dark places and found beauty, light, and the unmistakable presence of God in every corner. It has led to a joy that transcends even the hardest days. Not a "jumping up and down in delirious happiness" joy, but an abiding, steadfast joy in knowing that I am never alone. Jesus is there in the darkness, whispering words of comfort, peace, and goodness. So, no, I am not the Depression Lady. I'm the Joy Lady.

Familiar Ground

There are very few conclusions in this life. Events might change or end, but they are never really over. All you have learned and experienced in this Midnight are part of you. Even the really bad stuff. I don't want them to stick with you in a way that you re-experience them or feel shame. After all, you have been made new and are still being made new in Christ Jesus. At the same time, I would hate for you to lock up the hardest times of your life and throw away the key. They are too important to your story and they are way too important to God.

If Midnight has been long, hard, and painstaking, you might be tempted to close this chapter, leave it behind, and no longer look back on it once daylight arrives. But I hope you don't. I hope you keep your stones of remembrance out where you can see them. I hope that the gifts discovered in the dark places go into the light with you, that the brightness reveals even more about God's love, patience, and faithfulness to you.

If time is constantly moving, then you are never truly stuck. Things are always shifting. Changes might seem so incremental you don't notice them. Like when you look in the mirror and, one day, out of nowhere, an inch-long hair is protruding from your chin. How does it get there? You just looked yesterday and the coast was clear. Now? You look like your great-aunt Nelda who made those awful gelatin salads for every family function. Some changes are like that. Others, though, make you into someone stronger and braver than you could have ever imagined. Especially the changes that happen in the darkness. When you step into daylight, even great-aunt Nelda's gelatin salad won't scare you. You'll have been through something profound. Midnight will become familiar ground, which means you can be a light to others.

Once you are back in daylight, you can stand at the mouth of the cave and call out words of encouragement to those still there. You will be able help others traverse this time. You can speak with clarity on the gifts of the dark places because you've been there and you know them. You are not ashamed of them. Moreover, you can speak with humility and compassion because you know what it's like to have everything come undone.

You will be a beacon of encouragement to those in the struggle. You can testify to God's faithfulness. Like David, you will be able to look back at the mountains and valleys and see the Lord was with you. Your ears will be attuned to your Shepherd's voice so well you will not be tempted (or perhaps less tempted) to run at the first sign of trouble. You will be able to ignore your first instinct of fear and lean in to your Shepherd's voice. And you will trust His leading more than you trust your own eyes.

There will be a new sense of peace that pours over you even in the worst times of trouble. It will bless others. It will teach them how to attune their ears too. And maybe the next time the flock gets scared, it will be you who shows them where to run and to Whom they can run. And the next time the darkness descends and the skies grow black, you will not be so afraid. You will know that Midnight is the way of goodness and grace. You will know you can trust the darkness as surely as you trust the light, because God is with you in both. And you will know deep in your soul the light will always return.

Do You Believe It?

> I am convinced that neither death nor life, neither angels nor demons, neither the present nor the future, nor any powers, neither height nor depth, nor anything else in all creation, will be able to separate us from the love of God that is in Christ Jesus our Lord (Romans 8:38-39).

You are, first and foremost, a child of God, His pride and joy. His. He is enormously pleased with you. He delights in you. You have an Abba Father who loves you with an unending love. God wants to be with you so much He sent His only Son to die so you can live with Him in eternity. Jesus Christ, God's only Son, ensured that you would never be swept away by your brokenness and shame. Instead of leaving them on your shoulders to deal with, He took them upon His own instead. He made a way for you to be free from condemnation. He made sure there wasn't anything—sin, weakness, fear, darkness—that could take you away from the Father.

Everything that happens in your life influences, directs, and affects your personhood. You are never separate from your story. It is part of you. But so is God. And He takes the worst pieces of your story and, if you let Him, saturates them with His love and grace. Your deepest struggles are woven into your soul. Jesus Christ lives in them as much as He lives in the rest of your story. You are so beloved by Him that He wants all of you, even your heartaches. *Especially* your heartaches. There is nothing outside of His care.

Do you believe it? Does your heart want it? Even if part of you is skeptical, is there another part that thinks it could be true? Is hope sprouting up in you like a dandelion in the cracks of the sidewalk? This is the hope of Jesus Christ. This is His unending, inexhaustible invitation to you: "Come, follow Me." You might have a bunch of questions and be unsure about a lot of it. No matter. Jesus is calling:

"Come, follow Me." He will never force you. He isn't a bully. If you don't want to, you have that choice.

But if this book has given you any sense of strength or encouragement in the darkness, it is solely because of the light of Jesus Christ. Without Him, the words fall flat. They are without substance. They stop being true. Because suffering only leads to hope when it is under the care of Jesus Christ. He will lead if you want to follow. Let Him. Even if He leads you into the darkness, you can trust Him.

You don't need to put a lot of words around your desire for Him. Sometimes all you can do is grunt or groan in His direction. That's just fine. All He wants is your sincere desire to make Him the center of your life. If that is what you want, you can talk His ear off or write it in your journal. Or you can say out loud to Him, right now, "Let's begin." And it will.

The Radiant Midnight

> The Christian life is going to God…The difference is that each step we walk, each breath we breathe, we know we are preserved by God, we know we are accompanied by God, we know we are ruled by God; and therefore no matter what doubts we endure or what accidents we experience, the Lord will guard us from every evil, he guards our very life.
>
> —Eugene Peterson[2]

Jesus Christ invites you into the darkness of Midnight where He will teach you to surrender, not to pain or people or circumstances, but to Him alone. In surrendering to Him, you place yourself wholly in His arms. He will allow suffering, but He will never leave you alone in it. He will be with you every step of the way. Jesus will give your suffering deep meaning and value even when He doesn't remove it. He will make time work for your benefit and His glory. In every moment that passes, He is with you. On the days that crawl by and in the times that rush over you too quickly, He is making time submit to His perfect will. He invites you into silence, where you can explore the inner cathedral of your heart. You will find your Savior there too. He offers the practice of solitude, a regular time of communion with Him where He will whisper words of His pleasure and love. He is there among the people, within the community of others, where you will find camaraderie and comfort. You will find courage and strength enough to stand still in your circumstances, because He is casting out fear with His perfect love. You don't need to cower or run from the dark because the Lord is with you in it. You can be bold and courageous even when you can't see, because He is guiding you. And you can embrace hope in all ways, at all times, in every circumstance, because He transcends all of it. And Jesus will not leave. Ever.

The shared element in every gift of Midnight is the presence of God. He is the through line. He is the common denominator. You have not shed one tear, spent one sleepless night, had one difficult conversation without God being intimately aware of it. He has not taken His eyes off you. He hasn't blinked. And He is not going anywhere. You can be sure of God's presence more than any sunrise. Without Him, Midnight would just be darkness. Instead, it is beautifully, heartbreakingly, magnificently radiant because He is standing with you in the midst of it. Always.

We need both the sun and the moon. We need the storms and clear skies. We need daylight. And we need Midnight too. God does not eradicate our pain. He binds it. He honors it. He heals it. And He allows it—intentionally, carefully, and with immense love.

This life in Jesus Christ has been far different from what I imagined it would be. I believed He'd send me to a third-world country because He knew I'd be miserable there. He didn't. I thought He would heal me of my depression. He hasn't. I imagined He would behave in a way that made sense to me. Sometimes He does, but a lot of the time He doesn't. I asked Him to change my life, to hold me close, to love me and stay at the center of it. He did. I asked Him to be with me every moment of every day. He has.

Jesus Christ came into my life and it changed forever. He will do the same for you. In Him, you will find more joy and peace than you ever thought possible. You will develop a hope deep in your soul that transcends the darkness of grief, depression, and the very real struggles of this life. When you have Jesus Christ, you have a never-ending source of hope that bubbles up from the pit and refuses to be intimidated by circumstances or struggle, by depression or heartache.

He is the God of the grieving, the marginalized, the hurting, and the broken. He is the God of the popular and the talented. He is the God of the weak and afraid, the strong and courageous. He is the God of David, who embodied all of these things. He is the God of the mysterious and the known, of the sun and the moon, of the beginning and the end, of Midnight and of dawn. You can walk into the deepest darkness and be unafraid. In His unwavering presence, you are being made radiant.

MOONLIGHT MEDITATIONS

- Are there places where you are beginning to see daylight emerging?
- How has Midnight shaped your faith?
- What are the gifts of Midnight that you will take into the morning?

EVENING STROLL

- Take an early morning walk by yourself. Look at the trees and the birds and the beauty that surrounds you. Thank God for His abundance. Enjoy what you see in the light and say a prayer of gratitude to the God who made them all.

- Take a late evening walk alone. Look at the stars and the moon and the mysteries of what evening holds. Thank God for all of it. Enjoy what you discover in the darkness and say a prayer of gratitude to the God who is present in the midst of it all.

RESOURCES

The National Association of Mental Illness (NAMI)
www.nami.org
Helpline: 800-950-6264

Hope for Mental Health
www.hope4mentalhealth.com
949-609-8278

National Suicide Prevention Lifeline
www.suicidepreventionlifeline.org
800-273-8255

Celebrate Recovery
www.celebraterecovery.com

NOTES

Introduction

1. Dietrich Bonhoeffer, *Wonder of Wonders: Christmas with Dietrich Bonhoeffer*, trans. O.C. Dean Jr. (Louisville, KY: Westminster John Knox Press, 2015), 26.
2. H.D.M Spence and Joseph S. Exell (exposition by The Ven. Archdeacon Farrar, DD; homiletics by Rev. David Thomas, DD), *The Pulpit Commentary, Corinthians*, vol. 19 (New York: Funk & Wagnalls Company, 1950), 291.

Chapter 1: Welcome to Midnight

1. Gerald L. Sittser, *A Grace Disguised: How the Soul Grows Through Loss* (Grand Rapids, MI: Zondervan, 1996), 43.
2. See J.I. Packer, "John of the Cross: Spanish Mystic of the Soul's Dark Night," ChristianityToday.com, https://www.christianitytoday.com/history/people/innertravelers/john-of-cross.html.
3. John of the Cross, "Dark Night of the Soul" (poem).
4. See "Ra: The Sun God of Egypt," Ancient Egypt Online, http://www.ancient-egypt-online.com/egyptian-god-ra.html.
5. Timothy Keller, *The Meaning of Marriage: Facing the Complexities of Commitment with the Wisdom of God* (New York: Penguin Random House, 2013), 40.
6. William D. Mounce, ed., *Mounce's Complete Expository Dictionary of Old and New Testament Words* (Grand Rapids, MI: Zondervan, 2006), 1.
7. John of the Cross, "Dark Night of the Soul," chap. 12.

Chapter 2: Surrender and Salsa

1. Pat Conroy, *My Losing Season* (New York: Random House, 2002), 3.
2. Parker Palmer, *Let Your Life Speak: Listening for the Voice of Vocation* (San Francisco: Jossey-Bass, 2000), 41.
3. Dietrich Bonhoeffer, *The Cost of Discipleship* (New York: Touchstone, 1959), 51.

4. Mark Buchanan, *The Rest of God: Restoring Your Soul by Restoring Sabbath* (Nashville: W Publishing, 2006), 101.

5. Anthony Bozza, "Fighting the Good Fight, in the Name of Love and Rock & Roll," *Rolling Stone*, November 19, 2001, https://www.atu2.com/news/people-of-the-year-bono.html.

Chapter 3: No Thing Left

1. Michael Yaconelli, *Messy Spirituality* (Grand Rapids, MI: Zondervan, 2002), 15.

2. Henri Nouwen, *Turn My Mourning into Dancing: Moving Through Hard Times with Home* (Nashville: W Publishing, 2001), 7.

3. Voltaire (Francois-Marie Arouet), *Notebooks* (c1734–1750).

4. Brennan Manning, *Abba's Child: The Cry of the Heart for Intimate Belonging* (Colorado Springs: NavPress, 2002), 89.

5. C.S. Lewis, *The Problem of Pain* (New York: HarperCollins, 1940), 91.

Chapter 4: Long Starry Nights

1. Vincent van Gogh, "261: To Theo van Gogh. The Hague, Saturday, 9 September 1882," VanGoghLetters.org, http://vangoghletters.org/vg/letters/let261/letter.html.

2. "The Survivor Tree," 9/11 Memorial and Museum, https://www.911memorial.org/survivor-tree.

3. Henry Cloud, *Changes That Heal: How to Understand Your Past to Ensure a Healthier Future* (Grand Rapids, MI: Zondervan, 1992), 30.

4. "Vincent Van Gogh Biography," Van Gogh Gallery, https://www.vangoghgallery.com/misc/biography.html.

5. "Vincent Van Gogh: Starry Night," Van Gogh Gallery, https://www.vangoghgallery.com/painting/starry-night.html.

6. George Roddam, *This Is Van Gogh* (London: Laurence King, 2015), 64.

Chapter 5: The Silent God

1. T.S. Eliot, *The Waste Land*, 1922, public domain.

2. C.H. Spurgeon, *The Treasury of David: Containing an Original Exposition of the Book of Psalms*, 7 vols. (New York: Funk & Wagnalls, 1892) accessed at http://archive.spurgeon.org/treasury/treasury.php.

3. Ruth Hayley Barton, *Invitation to Solitude and Silence: Experiencing God's Transforming Presence* (Downer's Grove, IL: InterVarsity, 2010), 16.

4. Mother Teresa of Calcutta, *A Gift for God* (New York: Harper & Row, 1975), 83.

5. C.H. Spurgeon, *Treasury of David*, 88.

Chapter 6: Garbo, Loneliness, and the Unwavering Gaze of Grace

1. Fred Rogers, *The World According to Mister Rogers: Important Things to Remember* (New York: Family Communications, 2003), 31.

2. "The 'I Want to Be Alone' Quote," Garbo Forever, http://www.garbofor ever.com/I_want_to_be_alone.htm#Friends.

3. Brigit Katz, "The Profound Loneliness of Greta Garbo," Smithsonian .com, December 8, 2017, https://www.smithsonianmag.com/smart-news/ profound-loneliness-greta-garbo-180967417/.

4. Ibid.

5. C.S. Lewis, *Mere Christianity* (New York: HarperCollins, 1980), 227.

6. Aristotle, *Politics* 4.6-9.

7. A.W. Tozer, *The Pursuit of God: The Human Thirst for the Divine* (Camp Hill, PA: Christian Publications, 1993), 50.

8. Richard Foster, *Celebration of Discipline: The Path to Spiritual Growth* (New York: HarperCollins, 1998), 96.

Chapter 7: Poking Holes in the Darkness

1. A.A. Milne, *The House at Pooh Corner* (New York: Penguin, 1956), 150.

2. Eugene Peterson, *A Long Obedience in the Same Direction,* 2nd ed. (Downers Grove, IL: InterVarsity Press, 2000), 79.

3. Jaweed Kaleem, "Rick and Kay Warren Launch Saddleback Church Mental Health Ministry After Son's Suicide," HuffingtonPost.com, March 28, 2014, https://www.huffingtonpost.com/2014/03/28/rick-warren-mental-health_n_5051129.html.

4. Saddleback, "Hope for Mental Health," http://hope4mentalhealth.com.

5. Rick Warren, "My Son's Suicide and God's Garden of Grace," Premier Christianity, September 9, 2016, https://www.premierchristianity.com/ Blog/Rick-Warren-My-son-s-suicide-and-God-s-garden-of-grace.

6. Flannery O'Connor, *The Complete Stories of Flannery O'Connor* (New York: Farrar, Straus, and Giroux, 1971), 508.

Chapter 8: Fear Not

1. Stephen King, *Night Shift* (New York: Doubleday, 1978), xxiii.

2. Gavin de Becker, *The Gift of Fear: Survival Signals That Protect Us from Violence* (Boston: Little, Brown, 1997), 336-37.

3. Stephen D. Renn, ed., *Expository Dictionary of Bible Words: Word Studies for Key English Bible Words Based on the Hebrew and Greek Texts* (Peabody, MA: Hendrickson, 2005), 329.

4. See Alexander MacLaren, *The Book of Psalms*, Expositions of Holy Scripture (London: Hodder & Stoughton, 1908), and Albert Barnes, *Notes on the Bible* (1834), Sacred Texts, https://www.sacred-texts.com/bib/cmt/barnes/psa023.htm.

5. Anne Lamott, *Bird by Bird* (New York: Pantheon Books, 1994), 22.

6. "*David* (Michelangelo)," Wikipedia, https://en.wikipedia.org/wiki/David_(Michelangelo).

7. Ibid.

8. Eleanor Roosevelt, *You Learn by Living* (New York: HarperCollins, 1960), 41.

Chaper 9: Waiting for the Sun to Rise

1. Quoted in Deborah Solomon, "The Priest," *New York Times Magazine*, March 4, 2010, https://www.nytimes.com/2010/03/07/magazine/07fob-q4-t.html.

2. Brené Brown, *Daring Greatly: How the Courage to Be Vulnerable Transforms the Way We Live, Love, Parent, and Lead* (New York: Penguin, 2012), 68.

3. Frederick Buechner, *Secrets in the Darkness: A Life in Sermons* (New York: HarperCollins, 2006), 168.

Chapter 10: Welcome to Daylight

1. Brennan Manning, *Ruthless Trust: The Ragamuffins Path to God* (New York: HarperCollins, 2000), 37.

2. Eugene Peterson, *A Long Obedience in the Same Direction* (Downers Grove, IL: InterVarsity, 2000), 45.

ACKNOWLEDGMENTS

*Acknowledge: to own, avow or admit to be true,
by a declaration of assent.*

NOAH WEBSTER, *THE AMERICAN DICTIONARY
OF THE ENGLISH LANGUAGE*, 1828

Alot of what I've discussed in this book was difficult to acknowledge at times. But the people I'm writing to on these pages? Piece of cake. I "own, acknowledge, and admit to be true" that every one of them has helped to shape this book as well as my heart. I am forever grateful for both.

To Terry Glaspey, who had more confidence in my writing than I did. Thank you for your generosity in sharing my work. You are a gentle, artistic, and delightful presence in my life. Your love of the arts has made me remember my own. Thank you, thank you.

To my wonderful editor, Kathleen Kerr. Thank you for seeing the vision for this book and for understanding there is such a thing as a nondepressing book about depression. Your enthusiasm, support, astute edits, and sweet guidance have been an immense blessing. Thanks for helping me to discover, develop, and defend my voice as we worked together.

To Dr. Curt Thompson, who kindly and skillfully wrote the foreword to this book. Thank you for your generosity of time and talent toward this project. Your influence in my life is profound, and I'm just going to sound like a weirdo if I start to gush here.

To Nancy Stemme, who knows how to talk a girl off the ledge. You are a true Midnight companion. Your friendship is a bright star that shines in both the darkness of night and on the brightest of days, all the way from North Carolina. I love you.

To the extraordinary company of friends who surround me with love, attention, support, and grace. My Seasons family, my Sunday night group, and my walking, coffee, church, Cinespia, and sushi companions. To try to name you all is the beginning of panic that I might leave out a name that is written on my heart and yet has slipped my mind while writing this. It's an embarrassment of riches to have so many people to love. You know who you are. Thank you for being with me on this adventure.

To my family, who has seen my journey both up close and from the bleachers. Thanks for your support, love, and terrible singing on my birthday. I love you.

To Cole, my son who loves words like I do. Keep writing. You have important things to say. Your life is in the hand of God. There's no better place for it. I love you.

To Elizabeth, thanks for your patience when you heard me say for the umpteenth time, "Just five more minutes—I've got to finish this sentence." And thanks for waiting the next hour while I finished it. I love you, sweetheart.

To Danny, my love, my best friend, and my most enthusiastic supporter. Thank you for listening to these chapters as I wrote them. Thanks for making sure I was able to get away to write. Thanks for always being a safe place. I love you passionately, deeply, and enduringly.

To my Abba, Savior, Redeemer, and Friend: Jesus. Thank You for finding me in the darkness. Thank You for staying with me in those times when it returns. I am grateful for all of the parts of my story—every heartbreak, every dark corner, every new adventure, and every sunrise—because You are in all of them. You are the Radiance of Midnight and I am Yours.

ABOUT THE AUTHOR

Melissa Maimone writes with transparency, humor, and grace about the darkness of depression and the light of down-to-earth, authentic faith. Drawing from her lifelong battle with anxiety and depression, she speaks and writes to women facing similar struggles, offering hope in the midst of deep pain. She lives with her husband and children in Southern California.

https://www.**melissamaimone**.com

To learn more about Harvest House books and
to read sample chapters, visit our website:

www.harvesthousepublishers.com

HARVEST HOUSE PUBLISHERS
EUGENE, OREGON